Baby & Toddler Sleep Program

About the Authors

Dr. John Pearce is Professor of Child and Adolescent Psychiatry at the University of Nottingham. He has written a wide range of practical books for parents, plus numerous articles for magazines and newspapers. He speaks at national and international conferences on childcare issues and is a member of numerous professional organizations and committees.

Jane Bidder has been a journalist for the past 20 years and is a regular contributor to various magazines and newspapers. She and her husband have three children. They know all about sleepless nights! Jane represents the softer approach in the book.

Baby & Toddler Sleep Program

How to get your child to sleep through the night, every night

John Pearce, MD

with Jane Bidder

FISHER
BOOKS.

◡ For all sleepless parents ◡

Publishers: Bill Fisher
Helen V. Fisher
Howard W. Fisher

Managing Editor: Sarah Trotta

*North American
Editor:* Meg Morris

Cover Design: Lynn Bishop

*Book Design
& Production:* Randy Schultz

Illustrations: Cathie Lowmiller

Originally published as *The Baby and
Toddler Sleep Programme* ©1997 John
Pearce and Jane Bidder
by Vermilion, an imprint of Ebury Press
Random House
20 Vauxhall Bridge Road
London SW1V 2SA

Published by Fisher Books, LLC
5225 West Massingale Road
Tucson, AZ 85743-8416
(520) 744-6110
www.fisherbooks.com

Printed in the U.S.A.   10 9 8 7 6 5 4

**Library of Congress
Cataloging-in-Publication Data**

Pearce, John, 1940-
    Baby and toddler sleep program :
how to get your child to sleep through
the night, every night / John Pearce
with Jane Bidder. — North American ed.
    p.   cm.
    Originally published as : Baby and
toddler sleep programme. London :
Vermilion, 1997.
    Includes index.
    ISBN 1-55561-279-2
    1. Infants—Sleep—Popular works.
2. Toddlers—Sleep—Popular works.
3. Sleep disorders in children—
Prevention—Popular works.
I. Bidder, Jane. II. Title. III. Title:
Baby and toddler sleep program.
Rj506.S55P43 1999
649'.122—dc21   98-51783
                                    CIP

Note: The information in this book is true and complete to the best of
our knowledge. It is offered with no guarantees of the part of the
authors or Fisher Books. Author and publisher disclaim all liability in
connection with the use of this book.

Contents

Introduction

Pick up a selection of new-baby greeting cards and you're bound to find at least one with a cartoon of a typical new father. He stands in his pajamas with heavy, half-closed eyes ringed with exhaustion. In the background, a baby is screaming and—to drive the point home—the clock is pointing to 3 A.M.! We laugh because, as parents, we know how it feels firsthand.

New parents don't usually get much sleep. Suddenly, they are thrown from a normal, civilized adult life into a semi-comatose existence centered around a small baby who sleeps when they least want him to. (Please note that your baby is referred to as *he* throughout the text.)

As the baby grows, life doesn't always get much better. "Does your child sleep through the night yet?" is a much-discussed question and topic of conversation for parents of children from 6 weeks to 5 years of age—and even beyond. "Does he come into your bed at night?" is another question parents frequently ask each other.

One nurse I used to know would gleefully tell me that some governments used sleep deprivation as a form of torture in times of war. Her remark infuriated me at the time. I already knew lack of sleep was agony. What I needed was a practical book on how to cope with it and make my child sleep so I could get some rest.

Some babies do sleep regularly at night. Sometimes this is a matter of luck. But it also happens because their parents have *worked at it*. Yes, *you can* work on your child's sleep habits, just as you work at getting solids into his small reluctant mouth.

Sleep is one of the many habits you need to cultivate in your children. If you see it this way, it becomes a more achievable goal. Instead of relying on luck, you can train your child—and yourself—to have unbroken nights. But it will take time. And you may feel you don't have much of that at the moment.

If you persevere, you'll find there's a big payoff at the end. Teaching good sleep habits not only gets you the rest you need, but ensures your child gets rest too. And he'll have taken one more step toward *his* independence.

There's another plus—when you get your child into a regular sleep pattern, the whole family benefits. Not just you, but also your partner. It also helps your other children, who need your attention as well. New babies often make siblings jealous. And it's not surprising because new babies wake up often and are the center of attention.

So much for theory. What about the practice? How can you actually make a screaming baby or toddler go to bed and stay there? Read on and see!

Off to Sleep

Everyone needs sleep. Not just children, but parents too! It's amazing how much better you feel when you are rested. Somehow it's easier to deal with a difficult baby or child when you feel rested yourself.

Although you know you need sleep, how can that help you cope with a baby who wakes up every half-hour or a toddler who has decided that it's time to get up at 2 A.M.? You tell yourself you need sleep and that your child can be taught to stay happily in his bed. But how?

Sleep Habits

Sleep can't be turned on or off at will, but it is a habit and one of the first routines children need to develop. However, about 1 in 3 children under the age of 5 have disturbed sleep. And of these, almost a third have a serious problem.

The good news is that as children grow older, their sleep improves. By the age of 8, only 1 child in 10 has sleep problems. But 8 years is too long to wait until your child gets a good night's sleep! Unless, of course, you do something about it. That's where this book comes in.

Jeremy

Jeremy was 9 months old. He was the second child and his parents were astonished at how different he was from the firstborn. Jeremy cried a lot but it was not ordinary crying. He would scream and his little body would stiffen. He was difficult to feed, difficult to calm and fidgety. His mother thought she was doing something wrong. When she consulted the doctor he found nothing wrong with Jeremy.

Then Jeremy's mother read in a magazine that some children are born with a difficult temperament and they behave just like Jeremy. She was pleased to read that most of these children eventually settle down.

The article suggested that children like Jeremy benefit from routine in their life, with very clear limits set for their difficult behavior. At the same time they require extra loving care and close supervision.

Jeremy's parents put this into practice and gradually their persistence paid off. A year later everybody noticed an improvement in Jeremy's behavior. The bedtime routine was particularly helpful and evenings had become a peaceful time for everyone.

Why Don't Children Learn to Sleep Regularly?

❈ Your family doesn't have a regular bedtime routine. Following a routine helps you decide when, where and how to get your child to sleep.

❈ Children with strong emotions and irregular habits often find it hard to sleep without help. So do babies who had birth difficulties, babies with colic, children who are fed at night after 1 year, children over 6 months old who sleep in the same room with their parents and children whose parents are overworried or anxious.

❈ Overtired parents find it difficult to be firm and consistent. It's understandable. When you're under stress, you do things you wouldn't do if you felt more relaxed.

✧ You feel guilty, which can lead to overcompensation. You've been at work all day. So why can't your child stay up a little later than usual? Perhaps you yelled at your child for something during the afternoon. He's upset. If he stayed up a little later, you would have time to "make up."

✧ You're confused. Your doctor, mother-in-law, mother and friends all give you advice. Every piece of advice is different! What do you do?

Why Do Anything?

Why not put your child to bed when he wants to? He'll sleep whenever he wants, won't he? Yes, but will it fit in with when *you* want him to sleep? If your child isn't sleeping in a way that fits in with your way of life, everyone feels upset and irritable. Lack of sleep in children and adults leads to poor concentration and even depression.

Tired adults tend to slow down. But tired children often speed up and become hyperactive—not a good combination!

Tired adults tend to slow down. Tired children often speed up and become hyperactive—not a good combination! A tired, irritable child is not easy to deal with. And when you haven't had much sleep yourself, a tired child is even harder to handle.

Encouraging your child to develop good sleep habits actually brings you closer. Yes, really! You get to know his limits. You find out how tough he is and how he ticks. By negotiating a sleep pattern on *your* terms and not his, you encourage him to respect you as a parent. Some of this might sound old-fashioned and perhaps unfashionable, but you'll be surprised at how much respect and rest can help you both.

Help is at Hand

Every child and every family is different. What might have worked for a friend or for your mother-in-law may not work for you. While there are no right or wrong methods, some approaches are better and more effective than others.

If you're a working parent, consider keeping your child up during the evening to give you some extra time together. If that's the case, you also need to make sure your baby's or toddler's sleep needs are still being met. On the other hand, you might prefer a traditional early-bed approach so you can rediscover the meaning of the word "evening" and time for yourself!

This book aims to help you develop a plan tailor-made for *your* particular needs. There are two ways of doing this: tip-toeing at the shallow end or jumping in at the deep end. These days, the accent on childcare has become very informal. "Do what you feel is best" is the message from many parenting books, health-care providers and doctors. This works for some parents, but others need more definite guidelines. A return to specific, firm advice can help these parents. In each of the following chapters, we give strategies for a gradual approach and for a stricter, faster approach. In chapter 4, the Three-Day Sleep Plan guides you through one effective, fast-acting technique.

Which Approach?

Imagine yourself getting ready to hop into a cold swimming pool, cold bath or cold shower. As you shiver on the edge thinking about whether to go in slowly or quickly, you probably feel quite uncomfortable. But with experience most people find they prefer to get in quickly.

Jumping in at the deep end requires confidence. But the uncomfortable part is over quickly. If you stay shivering on the edge you may never get in at all, which won't do your confidence any good. The problem of going in at the shallow end is that the discomfort is prolonged. Many people who get in halfway decide to get out again.

Although generally it is best to jump in quickly at the deep end, this does not suit everyone. Some people prefer to take things gradually—making progress little by little. We encourage you to take the rapid approach, but if you prefer to do things more gradually, that's OK, too. It's your choice!

Some parents may find managing a rapid approach a little tough at first. But you achieve results faster if you begin when your child is still a baby. A slower approach is particularly useful for a child who has already developed bad sleep habits and needs to be coaxed into a bedtime routine.

Sleep and Rest

Going to bed means a lot more than simply *going to sleep*. It also means a *time to rest*. It's a chance for your child's body to stop moving so fast and to recharge his batteries.

The best proof is to watch your child when he's in that relaxed state just before drifting off to sleep or just after waking up. Who knows what is going on inside your baby's or toddler's mind when you catch him lying awake in his crib, gurgling to himself or staring at the mobile above him? Whatever it is, it's important to him! He's resting in bed and learning to enjoy the experience. Encourage this habit.

At bedtime, it's easy to forget the importance of simply *resting* the body. You can get very worked up about sleep. Because you feel so much better yourself when you've had enough sleep, it's natural to get emotional when you don't have enough or think your child hasn't had enough sleep: "Why isn't my child sleeping? What is wrong with him or us?" In fact, resting in bed is almost as good for you as sleeping. Resting in bed is something parents can control even though no one can make a child sleep.

It might help to see sleep as the first habit or stage in your child's growing-and-learning process. Picture it as the first rung of a ladder. You're there to help your baby or child onto the bar. Once he's there, he'll soon want to climb higher and higher.

Don't panic. Many parents naturally worry that their child will become ill if he doesn't get enough sleep. In fact, nature is too smart for that to happen: Instead, your child's body automatically sends him to sleep when he needs it. The problem is, this may not happen when *you* want it to! Think of all those toddlers who fall asleep in the back of the car on the afternoon ride to pick up older children from school and are then wide awake at 10 P.M. when their exhausted parents want to go to bed.

> Resting in bed is something parents can control even though no one can make a child sleep.

Teaching Self-Reliance

It helps to remember: Sleep is just another stage you go through to help your child become self-reliant. If you can catch your child early enough, it's possible to teach him not to be afraid of the dark. He can actually learn to enjoy lying in his bed in the dark—even if he hasn't closed his eyes.

Part of growing up is learning to be independent and confident when alone. If your child is able to learn how to be alone in bed at night in the dark, this helps him be confident during the day and more self-reliant.

See healthy sleep habits as an essential part of the process of helping your child grow. If you do, it becomes easier to diffuse the emotion involved. Instead of feeling guilty about putting your child to bed because you need time alone, remember you're doing *him* a favor, too. You're helping him learn to enjoy his own company. And you're enabling him to grow physically and mentally, because a child needs sleep as much as he does food.

> Resting in bed is almost as good for you as sleeping.

Safe and Sound

All parents worry about whether their children are safe. And this is just as important when they're tucked in bed. Bedrooms must be safe places, but unfortunately, this isn't always the case. Before putting your child to bed, make sure he is safe:

☆ In his crib or bed

☆ In his bedroom

☆ On the stairs, downstairs or anywhere else in the house where he is likely to wander during the night

Also ask yourself:

☆ Can he climb over the side of the crib?

☆ Can he get out of the window?

☆ If he wakes up before you in the morning, can he help himself to anything dangerous in the kitchen or bathroom?

☆ Can he pull anything within reach onto himself (such as a mobile, a lamp or curtains)?

We'll cover these points in greater depth in the following sections, but remember it is dangerous for your child to be on the loose while you are asleep.

Time for Yourself

Getting your child to bed is also crucial for you as a couple or, if you're on your own, for you as a person. Everyone needs time alone as much as they need sleep. It's a time to unwind and become a grown-up again instead of a parent who's busy keeping everyone else happy.

You need space and time to communicate and be together with your partner and friends. It's easy to forget how important this is. Your new baby is understandably the hub of your life. It seems selfish to think of yourself or what you'd like to do on Saturday night. But your baby will grow up eventually and make his own friends. He'll go to school, leave home and have babies himself. Where will you be then? It might be too late to rediscover your friends or even your partner. But, if you've permitted yourself to have "me time" from the beginning, you'll have the best of both worlds. You'll have treated yourself kindly, and you'll have created a self-reliant, happy child.

How Does Everyone Else Cope?

It's worth knowing how various cultures cope with sleep before you decide how to approach teaching good sleep habits in your own household. If other countries do it differently, why shouldn't you?

Italian and Spanish children, for example, frequently have midday naps (*siestas*) like their parents, and then stay up late. About half of African children sleep with their parents. Some say this helps them become confident because they are never alone. Others argue it delays the independence process.

Japanese babies often sleep in the parental bedroom until they are toddlers. If you choose to do the same, you are more likely to hear your baby if he's sick or upset. But one big disadvantage is your baby might find it difficult to sleep alone when he's older. Another problem is you are both less likely to sleep well without waking during the night. One of you is bound to disturb the other, either by turning over or by talking in your sleep.

The Japanese often share beds with their young children. So do 15% of British families. Some argue this can be dangerous because you may smother your child. Others maintain the child will be less likely to accept his own bedroom when he's older. Others argue the physical closeness of their parents gives young children vital comfort. The drawback is you could become a security blanket for your child. He may need your presence as constant reassurance.

Whenever you share a bed with someone, you also quickly pick up distressed emotions. While it might be useful for you to know what your child is feeling, to what extent do you want your child to know when *you* are upset?

Only you can determine the sleep style that's right for you. Each has advantages and disadvantages, which will be discussed later in this book.

What Sleep Patterns Are Normal?

Your friend's baby has been sleeping through the night since he was 2 weeks old, so what's wrong with *your* baby? The answer is simple: *nothing*. Raw statistics tend to drain your confidence as a parent. But it's natural to want to know what the rest of the world is doing.

Officially, 70% of babies sleep from midnight to 5 A.M. by the age of 3 months. This figure rises to 85% by the age of 6 months. But don't panic if yours is the only bedroom light on in your street at 2 A.M. Between the ages of 18 months and 2 years, half of those babies who had previously slept through the night suddenly start waking up. Maybe life is fair after all!

Tip . . ✶ ✶ ✶ ✶ ✶ ✶ ✶ ✶ ✶ ✶ ✶ ✶ ✶ ✶ ✶ ✶ ✶ ✶

Breastfed babies wake more frequently than bottlefed babies. The average age of sleeping through the night for a breastfed baby is 13 weeks compared to 11 weeks for bottlefed babies.

At 2 years, children also start resisting bedtime and resent being separated from their parents. It's not really surprising. How would you feel if someone pushed *you* off the couch and said, "You're on your own"? The trick is to help your child enjoy being on his own, just as you are enjoying your independence in another room.

When your child does fall asleep finally, he's likely to wake up—but that doesn't necessarily mean he'll get out of bed. Don't rush to his bedroom if you hear a slight rustling on the baby monitor. At the age of 2 months, for example, babies spend about

10% of the night awake and about 6% of the night awake when they reach 9 months. But parents are aware of this wakefulness only if they make frequent checks or sleep with the baby.

Research also shows that after 6 months, babies take longer to go to sleep—particularly deep sleep. The good news is many of these babies wake up once or even twice during the night and still manage to go back to sleep without help. It makes sense. You, and probably your partner, turn over in the night and maybe open your eyes for a few seconds. But that doesn't mean you want someone to rush up to you with an early-morning glass of juice.

The 6-month milestone is an important stage of development. This is when babies usually get into a clear daytime-awake and nighttime-asleep rhythm. It is also the time when they start to see themselves as individuals and show anxiety when separated from a parent.

> The 6-month milestone . . . the time when they . . . show anxiety when separated from a parent.

As children grow older, their sleep pattern continues to change. Newborn babies have phases of deep and light sleep, which alternate in cycles of about 20 minutes. That's why it's easier to wake up your baby with a slight noise one day, even though he didn't stir when you switched on the vacuum cleaner the day before. It's also why babies often fall asleep during a feeding; it doesn't mean they're not enjoying the milk!

These deep- and light-sleep cycles become steadily longer. By the time your child is 5 or 6 years old, they occur every hour or so. When your child becomes an adult, these cycles will last between 2 to 3 hours, which is why you might find yourself waking up most often between 1 and 2 A.M. and 4 and 5 A.M.

Mike

Mike was 1 month old. Since birth he had cried most of the time he was awake. He cried before feedings and after feedings, during the daytime and during the night. His parents were in their early 20s and Mike was their first child. They were particularly worried because Mike only seemed to sleep for short periods during the day and cried for a long time during the night.

Eventually, they took Mike to the doctor, who didn't find anything wrong. The doctor explained that some children cry more than others and that the normal sleep and

*waking cycle in the early days after birth is 20 to 30
minutes. The parents were reassured. They found if they
made quiet shushing sounds, wrapped him firmly in a
blanket or rocked him gently, Mike quieted quickly. They
also found if they left him to cry for gradually longer
periods before going to him, Mike was much more likely
to quiet himself.*

Building a Habit

During the first 6 months, your baby is still getting used to the
new world in which he's found himself. A brand-new baby
spends most of the day and night asleep. This isn't as good as it
sounds because he usually only sleeps deeply for 20-minute
bursts. If you are lucky, he learns quickly how to doze off again
after a short period of light sleep or waking.

By 3 months, children spend more time awake during the day
than during the night, but still
wake 4 or 5 times during the
night. They might stay quiet or
they might try out those new
lungs of theirs!

> Most children sleep through the
> night at 6 months. Now is the time
> to put your sleep plan into operation.

By about 6 months, however, parents are presented with a
great opportunity. Most children sleep through the night at 6
months. Now is the time to put your sleep plan into operation. If
you leave it to later than this, the job will be much harder. The
stable wake and sleep cycles, which most 6-month-old children
begin to develop, break down by 2 years if you haven't established a regular sleep routine.

Jennifer

*Jennifer was 3 months old and had developed the habit of
crying in the evening. Her parents found this particularly
distressing because they both felt tired themselves. They
wondered if Jennifer actually knew this was a time when
they would do almost anything to keep her quiet! Their
pediatrician explained it is normal for babies between 1
and 3 months of age to cry more in the evening than at
any other time. They were also reassured to hear most
babies cry less and less after the age of 3 months, and*

excessive crying before that age does not predict crying at a later stage.

It was less comforting for the parents to hear crying at night tends to increase again between the ages of 9 months and 1 year. They learned that, even if they got Jennifer into a good nighttime sleep pattern, she probably would go through a phase of unsettled sleep once more between the ages of 2 and 3. (See chart below.)

This information made Jennifer's parents more determined than ever to get her into a good sleep routine early.

Babies experience various crying stages. Excessive crying before the age of 3 months does not predict continued crying in later stages.

Crying Frequency	
Age	**Stage Characteristics**
Between 1 and 3 months old	Frequent crying at night
After 3 months old	Crying at night decreases
Between 9 months old and 1 year old	Crying at night increases
Between 2 years old and 3 years old	Unsettled sleep patterns

Sleep is part of the daily routine, just like toilet training, feeding and dressing. It is a habit, and good habits don't always develop naturally. Sometimes they have to be created by regular training and routine. And guess who's the trainer!

Building a habit—especially a sleep habit—may be hard work. But when you achieve it, life becomes a lot easier. Think of learning to use a typewriter. At first, the letters seem to be all over the place, but then you learn to use the right keys in the right order. Eventually, through practice, you get a good result—you type quickly and accurately. The same principle applies to sleep training.

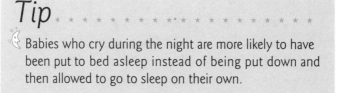

Tip *

Babies who cry during the night are more likely to have been put to bed asleep instead of being put down and then allowed to go to sleep on their own.

Methods That Work

In the rest of this book, we deal with the six major sleep stages: getting your child to bed, staying in bed, going to sleep, staying asleep, sleep disorders (such as nightmares) and sleep behaviors, such as wetting the bed. We suggest a variety of methods for each: It's up to you to try them out to see which works for you.

Sometimes, you'll want to mix-and-match. A rapid approach in one section may appeal to you, and a more gradual approach from another part of this book might also do the trick. There are no hard-and-fast rules in this business, which your baby knows all too well! But some "tricks" will work better than others.

Putting your child to bed and getting him up in the morning is a good way to learn about him. You discover what works well and what he doesn't like. You find out how he reacts to pressure or how he behaves when things don't go his way. You see how independent and capable he is. You also find out more about yourself and how you cope with your child.

> Putting your child to bed and getting him up in the morning is a good way to learn about him.

How well, after all, do you know your little one? Can you tell when he is genuinely upset or when he is simply angry because he can't have you to himself all the time? How easily can he control you? Are you training him, or is he training you?

Tip ★

There is no benefit in giving babies solid food to encourage sleeping through the night.

Your Child's Sleep Patterns

Before you begin the Three-Day Sleep Program (see chapter 4) or your own program devised from this book, complete the following questionnaires. The questions and exercises help you clarify what your child is *really* doing at night. The questionnaires also help you realize how your own behavior influences your child. The questionaires on pages 14 to 20 are provided for your personal use. Photocopy the forms as you need them.

Sleep Questionnaire and Daily Checklist

What is your child *really* doing at night? For example, you might think your toddler is waking up every night at 3 A.M. but if you make a note of it, you might find he wakes up 5 nights out of 7 and the time varies. Find a pattern, and you have another clue to help you solve a sleep problem.

That's what this is all about—uncovering patterns and changing behavior accordingly. There are no wrong answers. This questionnaire is provided to make you more aware of what you and your child are doing at night.

You might think, for instance, that you put your child to bed at roughly the same time each night; say, 7 P.M. But if you fill in the Sleep Questionnaire every evening for a week, you might find the time varies by as much as an hour from day to day.

> This is all about uncovering patterns and changing behavior accordingly. There are no wrong answers to the Questionnaire.

Children's bodies are like ours. They have an internal alarm clock. When you have gone to bed 1 or 2 hours later than normal, you might not feel very rested. And a child won't either—even a young one. Adults can quickly get into a routine of waking just before the alarm goes off in the morning. Children also rapidly develop waking habits, but not always when you would like them to.

When you've filled out the questionnaire, read it again. Let your partner read it. Ask yourself if you can learn anything from your answers. For example, does your child's late-afternoon nap prevent him from resting when you put him to bed at 7 P.M.? Would it help if you moved his nap to the early afternoon?

The Daily Checklist is designed to help you keep track of your child's sleep patterns. Photocopy it so you have a form for each day and each child in your family for one week. (Use a different checklist for each child.)

Parent's Behavior Checklist

Believe it or not, the way *you* behave can decide how well your child sleeps! Just like the Sleep Questionnaire, the Parent's Behavior Checklist has no wrong answers. You don't score points—or lose any—according to your responses. But it does help you think about what you're doing. And because of that, you may decide to try doing certain things differently. As you read through the book, refer back to the questionnaires. Add any new comments you think of at the bottom in the space provided. Then compare the advice in the book to what you are doing now, and see which patterns to change.

Sleep Questionnaire

Child's Name _____ Age _____ Date _____

Sleep Arrangements

1. Is he in a crib or a bed?

    _____

2. Where does your child sleep?

    _____

3. Does this location change during the evening? For example, does he fall asleep in your bed and then have to be moved into his own? Or does he fall asleep in his bed and then come into your bed during the night?

    _____

4. Does he share a bedroom with a parent, brother, sister or someone else?

    _____

5. Does he stay in his crib/bed without trying to get out? Does he get out of bed during the night? If yes, where does he go?

    _____

Bedtime Routine

1. How do you get him to sleep? Describe the routine.

    _____

2. How long before bedtime do you start this routine?

    _____

3. Is there a fixed bedtime? If so, at what time is it?

    _____

4. If you have other children, do they go to bed at the same time?

    _____

5. Does your child nap during the day? If so, at what time and for how long?

    _____

Continued . . .

6. Does he feel sleepy during the day but doesn't take a nap?

_____

Falling Asleep

1. What kind of aids does your child need to go to sleep? (for example, stuffed animal / blanket / toy / you)

_____

2. Is he afraid of the dark? If so, are you? Do you leave a light on or the bedroom door open?

_____

3. Is he distressed when he's left alone in his crib / bed? If so, what do you do?

_____

4. Does he head-bang or rock his body?

_____

5. Do you stay with him while he goes to sleep, or do you leave him to fall asleep on his own? How long do you have to stay?

_____

6. How long does it take him to go to sleep?

_____

7. Does he rest quietly on his own before going to sleep?

_____

Sleep Disturbances

1. Does he wake up during the night? How many times? Is there a pattern? For example, does he wake up at roughly the same times?

_____

2. What problems does he have when he's asleep? When did they start and how often do they occur?

_____

Continued . . .

3. Does he have nightmares? How often and at what time in the night?

_____

4. Does he cry in the night? How often and for how long?

_____

5. Does he wet the bed in the night? Is there a pattern to this or an approximate time? How often?

_____

6. Does he sleepwalk? Is there any obvious reason for this? How often does he sleepwalk and at what time in the night?

_____

7. Does he snore?

_____

8. Does he fall out of bed?

_____

Morning Routine

1. What time (roughly) does he wake up?

_____

2. Do you have to wake him up or does he wake up by himself?

_____

3. What does he do then? (for example, play/come into your bed/turn on the television)

_____

Other comments:

Daily Checklist

Child's Name _____ Date _____ Day of the Week _____

Daytime Routine

Event	Time	Comments
Woke up		
A.M. Nap		
P.M. Nap		
Other		
Other		

Bedtime Routine

Event	Time	Comments
Picked up room		
Bath		
Other		
Story / Prayers		
Other		
Lights out		

Nighttime Disturbances

Event	Time	Comments
Nightmares		
Bedwetting		
Woke up crying		
Came in our room		
Other		
Other		
Other		

Parent's Behavior Checklist

1. How much sleep do you get? Is it enough? Do you feel tired during the day/evening/both?

    _____

2. How many adults are involved in putting your child to bed?

    _____

3. Does your partner come home late?

    _____

4. Does his or her arrival disturb your child's sleep routine?

    _____

5. How do you react if your child cries in his crib/bed or tries to get out?

    _____

6. If you have other children, how do you look after them while you're getting the younger ones to bed?

    _____

7. Do you give up if your child won't sleep and let him stay with you in the evening?

    _____

8. Are you consistent when you say "yes" or "no" to your child?

    _____

9. a. Do all the adults at home have the same ideas as you about your child's sleep routine?

    _____

    b. Do these differences of opinion make you argue over your child's bedtime?

    _____

10. If your partner thinks you should put your child to bed in a different way, have you let him or her try?

    _____

11. Does your child prefer you or your partner to put him to bed?

    _____

Continued . . .

12. What would happen if one of you left the house and the "less-experienced" person had to do it?

_____

13. a. Does your child come into your bed at night?

_____

   b. Do you or your partner mind?

_____

14. Does your child's nighttime behavior interfere with your sex life?

_____

15. a. Do you check your children when they're asleep? How often?

_____

   b. Does it disturb them?

_____

   c. What would happen if you didn't check them so regularly?

_____

16. How often do you wake up during the night? What do you do then? (for example, turn over / lie awake / check the children / wake up your partner)

_____

17. If your child wakes up early, do you take him back to bed / let him come into yours / get up and start the day early?

_____

18. Do you reward your older toddler / child if he's rested through the night and stayed in his own bed? If so, how?

_____

19. Have you asked for professional help on your child's sleep habits? What was the most / least useful advice you'd pass on to another parent?

_____

20. If you were a new parent again, what would you do / not do when trying to get your child to sleep?

_____

Continued . . .

21. Are you a relaxed parent or do you worry a lot? Are most of these worries unnecessary? Is there a particular reason for your concerns? (for example, stillbirth / miscarriage / SIDS / depression / general anxiety / insecurity)

_____

22. a. What do you remember from your own childhood about sleeping and going to bed? Were you afraid of the dark?

    _____

    b. Have you ever left someone else in charge—apart from your partner—to put your child to bed? What happened?

    _____

23. If not, why not? Are you worried your child won't let anyone else do the job?

_____

24. Is there general family stress that might affect your child?

_____

25. Who in the family is affected by your child's inability to sleep well?

_____

26. Do you have a way of making it clear to your child that you are serious and mean what you say?

_____

27. Can your child tell from your face that you mean business and he must do what you say?

_____

Other comments:

2

Safety and Getting Your Child to Bed

For your own peace of mind, you need to know your child is safe when you leave him in his room at night—just as you make sure he is safe during the day. How safe is your child's bedroom? Because he is alone in his room for long periods, you need to make sure he can't hurt himself. He must be totally safe in his room.

Safety

Study the following checklist to make sure his room is child-proof. It's easy to become overly worried about safety. One of the best ways to deal with this fear is to make sure your child is as safe as possible.

Crib or Bed

Does it conform to U.S. and Canadian safety standards? (See the appendix for more information.) Beware of old or secondhand items with loose parts a child could swallow or toxic paint he could eat.

Mattress

Does it fit snugly into the bedframe? If there's a gap, your child might become trapped.

Crib Bumpers

Could your child get tangled in the crib bumpers and be injured if he tries to get out? If you're worried, remove them.

Bed

When your child has just graduated to a bed, buy a bed guard (a temporary bumper designed to prevent children from falling out of bed). Make sure it complies with U.S. and Canadian safety standards and doesn't trap your child. (See the appendix for more information.) Alternatively, place blankets or a comforter on the floor next to the bed so if your child falls out, he won't hurt himself.

Sleep Position

If your child is still a baby, make sure he sleeps on his back and not his front. (Experts don't all agree what causes sudden infant death syndrome, but sleep position and temperature control seem to be important factors.)

Windows

Could your child climb out of the window? Childproof the windows if necessary.

Heating

Never leave on an electric heater in your child's room. He could interfere with it and cause a fire or be burned by the heating element. If you don't have central heating or your bedrooms are drafty, dress your child in warm layers according to the weather. Remember: It's just as dangerous for children, especially young babies, to be too warm as it is to be too cold. Check by placing your hand against your child's cheek. It should feel the same temperature as your own body.

Toys

Could your child put a cord from a toy around his neck? Toys with strings and cords need to be put safely away before bedtime. Also, balloons can easily deflate or pop, and your child could choke on the deflated pieces. All toys should be age-appropriate for your child.

Furniture

Is the dresser in your child's room stable? Could he pull it over on himself? Are there chairs or other furniture he might try to climb on and either pull over or fall off of?

Door Locks

Is it possible for your child to lock himself inside his room? If so, remove the lock.

Baby Monitor

A plug-in monitor helps you hear if your child is in trouble. But use it with caution. Don't run in every time you hear him turn over! This only encourages him to wake up more often. Instead of keeping the monitor on all the time, turn it on briefly from time to time to check on him, and then turn it off again.

Electrical Outlets

Cover electrical outlets with childproof caps.

Pillows

Pillows can be dangerous for young babies because they can interfere with breathing. Young children don't need a pillow. As a general rule, wait until your toddler is between a year and 18 months old at the earliest. Your child's first pillow should be firm and thin.

How To Check on Your Baby's Safety

It is *absolutely essential* for parents to know their child is safe. Parents check their newborn babies very frequently. As time passes, they are able to wait longer before checking. Parents learn to "read" their child to know whether he is OK or not, and so will you.

The more frequently parents check on children during the night, the more likely the children are to cry and be disturbed. Parents must be able to check on their child's safety in bed without disturbing him. Here are some suggestions:

A baby monitor—switch it on only to check that your baby is breathing quietly and peacefully. Then switch it off again.

The door cracked open slightly—so you can see your child in bed through the gap without entering the room.

A mirror or a glass-framed picture—positioned on the wall to help you peek into the room from the hall and see your child in bed.

A dimmer switch or a flashlight—avoids the need to turn on a bright light.

Crouch when you look in—so your head is not where your child would expect it to be when you open the door to his room.

Put a peephole in the door—so you can keep the door closed when you check on your child.

Bedtime Routine

Getting your child to bed may sound like the easy part. It can be easy, but it is also important because it is the cornerstone of your child's sleep routine. If you do it the right way for you and your child, you are more likely to succeed at your goal of getting a good night's rest and having a happy child during the day.

Think of it from a child's perspective: Picture yourself happily reading a book or watching a favorite television program, when suddenly someone yanks you up, and says, "Time for bed!" Then this person marches you straight to your bedroom. Chances are you won't feel calm or relaxed enough to rest, let alone sleep.

> Children love ritual. They enjoy the same things over and over again, like a favorite story. It makes them feel secure.

Children, like adults, need a wind-down period to bridge the gap between an active day and a quiet night.

Simply saying, "Go to bed!" rarely works. An older child picks up on your desperation. A baby senses your distress and becomes upset himself. Instead of issuing commands, remember the key word "routine." Picture it in big letters over the bedroom door, and believe in it.

Over the past few years, "routine" has become an old-fashioned and sometimes unfavorable term, yet it is the building block for positive, well-adjusted children. Getting your child into a good bedtime routine makes a surprising difference.

You have an internal clock. If you're used to going to bed at 10 P.M. and you suddenly have a week of going to bed at 11 P.M. instead, you'll feel tired and irritable. A child has his *own* internal clock. The only difference is, he's waiting for you to set his. If you don't do it, he'll set it for himself—to a time that doesn't fit your schedule!

Young Babies' Routines

Young babies need to find their own routines. Start putting them to bed when you sense they are just about to fall asleep. Watch for warning signs such as droopy eyelids or their special, tired cry. Then head for the crib. If he wakes up as you put him down, do the following:

☆ Make low shushing sounds

☆ Hum

☆ Stroke his head gently

Juan

Juan's mother had not slept well since Juan's birth 5 months earlier. This was partly due to Juan crying during the night. She felt progressively more tired and miserable. She couldn't cope with Juan, and felt she was letting down her husband.

When he woke up, he cried until somebody came to him. His parents tried everything to calm him and stop his crying. They cuddled him, rocked him quietly, sang lullabies, hummed, put a clock with a loud tick by him, carried him in their arms and massaged him. Sometimes one thing would work and sometimes another would.

In desperation, she called her doctor for help. The doctor diagnosed her with postpartum depression, which usually responds well to medical treatment. Soon she felt much better. Unfortunately, Juan was already in a set routine of waking up during the night.

Because Juan's mother was feeling better and there was nothing wrong with Juan, they decided to let Juan cry. Both parents felt it was too difficult to ignore him altogether, so they decided to let him cry for 3 minutes the first day and delay going in by 1 minute each day. This worked well. Juan started to get the message after a week and was into a good sleep routine 3 weeks later.

Older Babies' and Toddlers' Routines

You can start a sleep routine when your child is 6 months old. It helps him learn to sleep well later on. Even little ones learn to recognize signs such as dimming the lights and singing a lullaby.

A young toddler can help put his toys away in the toy box to prepare for bedtime.

Start by getting your child ready for bed at the same time every evening. This isn't always easy if you have other children with full schedules. Aim for a reasonable time that allows some leeway for unexpected snags. The routine you follow will depend on you and your circumstances. But here are some examples in chronological order.

Suggested Bedtime Routine

1. Allow a suitable period of time—at least 30 minutes—to let your child's dinner digest before you start the countdown for bed.

2. Always follow the same routine. Do everything in the same order and with the same timing.

3. Calm down excited games and turn off the television.

4. Close the curtains and dim the lights.

5. Encourage toddlers to pick up toys as a winding-down process.

6. Run the bath. If he's old enough, ask your child to get his towel and pajamas ready. Enjoy a fun bath time but avoid rowdy games that excite him and wake him up.

7. Is he used to having a drink of water by his bedside? If so, make sure it's in place ahead of time: He can't hop out of bed again while you're getting it.

8. Encourage an older child—2 years and older—to look at the clock. Use the clock in the living room to signal the start of the bedtime routine. Use the clock in the bedroom to signal the time to be in bed. A novelty design, such as an animal whose eyes move as the clock ticks, might appeal to your little one and make this exercise fun.

9. Most children can't read the time until the age of 7 or 8. But you could put a marker on the clock to show bedtime. Help him read the time and then reinforce it with, "Yes, it's 6 P.M. Bedtime!" This makes the *clock* the "bad guy"— instead of you. The *clock* decides it's time to turn out the light and go to sleep.

10. Tuck a favorite doll or toy into a doll's bed. Say, "See, time for doll's bed. Time for you to go to bed, too." Tuck your child in bed and read a story together. Say your prayers together. Make sure he has his special bedtime toy or stuffed animal that's safe to have in bed with him. (See the safety checklist on pages 21-24.)

11. Sing a soft lullaby. Even older children enjoy this, especially if you've always done it. It's a reassuring ritual. You don't have to be a great singer or even sing in tune for this to be calming. The familiar sound is the important thing.

12. Say your special goodnight phrase. This might be simple, like "Good night, sleep tight." Keep it the same every time.

13. Keep the time you spend with your child when he is in bed to a minimum. The longer you stay, the more likely he is to protest when you leave, and cry during the night.

14. Turn off the bedroom light. Leave the hallway light on if necessary. Then leave the room and shut the door. Remember: You have already made sure the room is safe and you can use the baby monitor to check that everything is all right.

Special "Magic" Bedtime Phrases

Use special bedtime phrases when you put your child to bed and again if he wakes up at night. Familiar words soothe him:

- Nighty-night.
- Good night, little one.
- Shhhh, shut your eyes. Goodnight.
- Sweet dreams.
- God bless, sleep well.

Common Questions and Issues

Here are some common questions parents have about the bed-time routine. Each question is followed with an individual answer.

"I mention the word 'bedtime' and my toddler gets very upset. I can't cope with his outbursts and all those tears. What can I do?"

Use the clock. It's not *you* who says it's bedtime—it's the *clock*. There's nothing you can do about it. Don't make a big issue about bedtime. Treat it as an immovable event, like suppertime. The idea is: "You need to eat—*and* you need to go to bed."

If your child is old enough, you could talk about other children going to bed and maybe animals, too. If it's dark, use that as evidence it's time to go to bed. Don't reason too much with your child—he might win the argument!

"My 2-year-old uses delay tactics! When I say it's time for bed, my 2-year-old and her 4-year-old sister beg me for one more story or one more television program. I feel mean saying 'no.' Should I stick to my guns?"

Definitely. Use the bedtime routine as your yardstick. You're lost without it! After all, when does "one more" stop? It's like crossing the street safely: Your child needs to learn when you say "no," you mean it. It isn't cruel—it's merely setting boundaries. Children like and need to know how far they can go. Setting boundaries is another way of helping them feel secure. (Even if they don't seem to appreciate it at the time!)

Samantha and Josh

Samantha, 3, and her brother Josh, 5, didn't like to go to bed. They were particularly good at delay tactics. Their favorite was, "just one more" (one more game, one more story, one more page, and so on). If this strategy didn't work, they had a number of trump cards up their sleeves. These included "I need to go to the toilet," "I feel sick" and "My tummy hurts."

Their father was a doctor who worked long, irregular hours. The children never knew when he would be home. They wanted to stay up to see him. The father thought it was a good idea, but the mother didn't, because it always led to their protests and refusal to go to bed. Bedtime had become a nightmare. On the advice of another parent, they decided to start a regular bedtime routine. The routine led the children step by step from brushing their teeth to saying goodnight in a predictable way. They timed each stage exactly by the clock. This meant their father was not always home at bedtime. He did manage to change his schedule to be home more often.

It didn't take long for the children to start reminding their parents of the schedule. Instead of controlling their parents by trying to delay bedtime, they started to insist that their parents keep to their side of the agreement and stick precisely to the routine. Their parents were delighted because their evenings were so much easier.

"Our family life is too complicated to have a routine. We have three children and there's so much going on. What should we do?"

Life is too complicated *not* to have a routine. You can choose not to have a routine, of course, but your evenings will remain chaotic. Cut down on the different things you do in the evening. It's easy to overextend yourself and have too many activities going on for "the children's sake." Maybe it's worth making some sacrifices to create a calmer evening. Once you've established a routine, you can bend the rules once in a while.

"My 4-year-old won't let me help her get ready for bed. She won't get out of the bath or brush her teeth. What should I do?"

Make it a game. Keep the game focused, but make it fun. Use counting. For example, say, "Let's count to 10 and by then you should be out of the bath." If that doesn't work, pull out the plug and tell her you'll turn on the cold water. Make sure you carry out your "threat" if she doesn't cooperate. For children 5 and older, try counting in another language. The novelty might inspire them to participate.

Another game is to start a running commentary ("Emily is getting out of her bath and she's brushing her teeth"), but make sure you say each phrase as she does the action. She'll join in the fun and want to go faster. (See the Uncooperative Child section on pages 35-36.)

"My son insists on having a lot of stuffed animals in his bed. There's hardly room for him. If I make a fuss, he won't go to bed. What should I do?"

You're right. There won't be enough room for him. He won't feel comfortable, and that could disturb his sleep pattern. Suggest to your child he find one or two special "sleeping stuffed animals" who are only for bedtime. You could find special toy pajamas for them to make their bedtime more of an occasion.

"The bedroom door has to be left open. My 2-year-old insists on it. Is this wrong?"

A wide-open door gives the message that it's only safe outside. It suggests that life is *so* dangerous that Mommy and Daddy need an open door so they can rush in at any time! *Start* with a shut door so children won't learn to be scared to be alone.

If they have already learned to be scared, then gradually close the door little by little over a period of time until there's a small gap or maybe none at all. You could make this into a game for older children: Mark the floor with a goal for each day. On Monday, it will be open *this much*—on Tuesday, *this much*, and so on.

"My 18-month-old only goes to bed if I lie down with him. I don't have time to do this because we have a new baby. What can I do?"

Children do need comforting. It's natural. But are you going to be his sole comfort for the next 5 years? If you lie down with your child every time he goes to sleep, he's more likely to miss you when he wakes up. (Also see chapter 4 for more about Letting Your Child Cry.)

If you feel you have to stay with your child, try the gradual approach of sitting by his bed for shorter and shorter periods of time.

Dimitri

Dimitri was 4 and his father had left the family the year before. Naturally Dimitri's mother was upset about what had happened, and Dimitri missed his father. Neither he nor his mother had been sleeping well, and they found they got a lot of comfort from being together in the evening. Dimitri would eventually fall asleep at about 10 P.M. and his mother would carry him upstairs into her own bed. When she didn't, he would wake up screaming during the night. Dimitri was often restless at night. He frequently woke up his mother, and she was exhausted.

She was so desperate she even asked her doctor for sleeping pills. The doctor explained that although medication can help people sleep during a short crisis, later it would be more difficult to sleep without it, because sleeping pills can be addictive. Instead, he told her to get Dimitri into a good sleep routine and move him into his own bedroom.

In spite of her efforts, Dimitri's mom was unable to get him into a routine. He was difficult and demanding. She felt it was cruel to force him to do something that upset him—particularly after his father's departure. She decided to return to the old routine and allow Dimitri to sleep with her. The problems continued.

Finally, Dimitri's mother decided she must get Dimitri into a better sleep habit and put him to bed in his own room. She got the support of her mother and several friends who lived nearby. They all worked together to help her stick to the plan. It was particularly helpful to use an alarm clock to mark Dimitri's bedtime. Dimitri would look at the clock and suddenly race to his room, leaping into bed just before the alarm went off.

"What can I do during daylight savings? My children won't go to sleep when the clocks change in the spring and fall. They say it's too light in the spring, and they are too tired in the fall."

They're good excuses, yet adults can do it—even animals. Your dog may not be "used to" going to bed at 8 P.M. when it was 9 P.M. last night. But he does it. Millions of children all over the United States and Canada do it. And so can yours. Two suggestions

- ✦ Buy a curtain liner. Use it to make bedroom curtains thicker in the summer so the room will be darker.
- ✦ Rely on the clock. It may feel like 6 P.M., but the clock says 7 P.M., so it *is* bedtime.

"What should we do on vacation? It's difficult to get our young ones (under 5 years old) to sleep on vacation when the routine is disrupted. We have the same problem on the weekends, especially if we get back late from a day out. What should we do?"

Stick to the routine wherever you are. Modify it slightly if need be. For example, if you go out to dinner, go early so you are back before your child's bedtime. This may sound restrictive but it is worth the effort to maintain the pattern you have worked hard to create. It's difficult to keep to your normal routine while on vacation. Use parts of the routine, like the goodnight phrase or the bath-time ritual to help maintain the established bedtime pattern.

The same applies when you have guests at home. It might be tempting to let your children stay up, but it could hurt their new routine. You can do something different once in a while *after* their routine is firmly established.

"What do I do with my other children? How can I include all of them in the routine?"

Most parents who have one child wonder how they'll cope. When they have two children, they realize how easy it was when they had just one! Often they give up completely on setting bedtimes after the third child. They think it's too complicated! This is a mistake—for parents and for older children who need time alone with you, too. Graded bedtimes are a good way to help each child feel different and special.

If you have two or more children, you can still stick to the earlier suggested routine. Stagger the times. Start with the youngest. Once he's resting in bed, deal with the second child. (If you have trouble keeping the younger ones in bed, see chapter 3 for help.)

Alternatively, you might find it more practical to start the bedtime routine with all the children together: Put the older ones into their beds with a book while you handle the youngest. When the youngest is settled, you can move on to story time with the middle child and then the oldest (provided you have any voice left).

Treat children differently because the more you treat them the same, the more jealous they are likely to be of each other. If you spend exactly the same time with each child at bedtime, they count the seconds and notice any slight difference in the time you spend with them.

Stagger privileges like bedtime or lights out by ages so the oldest has the "best" deal— this helps him not feel jealous of the younger ones. The oldest is the only child who knows what it is like to have individual parental care and attention. If the younger ones complain about their earlier bedtime, remind them that they are moving up the ladder. Tell them, "This time next year you'll be able to stay up 15 minutes later, too!"

> Stagger privileges like bedtime or lights out, so the oldest has the best deal.

Remember: Once your children are in bed, it is best not to spend too much time with them. The longer you spend, the more awake your child will be. After all, would you want to go to sleep if someone interesting were sitting at the end of your bed talking with you?

"My husband ruins my routine. He comes home just when I'm getting our baby and toddler to bed. He wants to see them but I want to stick to what we're doing. Am I being unfair?"

It's natural for your husband to want to see his children after a day at work. You, on the other hand, have probably seen enough of them! Bedtime can be just as important for the parent's routine as for the child's.

Sit down with your partner and work out what is best for the family. Explain why the bedtime routine is so important. If your partner can't come home in time to see the children before their bedtime, suggest he take care of them on his own for an hour or so on the weekend. Maybe he could change his work hours. Is it really necessary to work late? How about starting earlier and finishing earlier?

If there still are problems, have him walk in your shoes—leave the children with your partner for the day (on the weekend).

Come back just as he is putting them to bed. The partner at home will discover it's not much fun.

Don't feel guilty that your child doesn't see both you and your partner at the end of the day. It would be nice if he saw both of you, but that isn't always possible. Instead of feeling guilty, you can

- ⭐ Call your partner after supper so your toddler can say goodnight.

- ⭐ Encourage your toddler to draw a special picture for your partner for when he comes home.

- ⭐ Give your partner a full account of what happened during the day. It is important for both parents to know what goes on each day. A child feels loved and supported when he knows his parents communicate about him.

When the Routine Isn't Working

If you've tried to establish a bedtime routine but it still isn't working, think about why it's not succeeding. Is it because

- ⭐ **The adults in the house don't agree on bedtime rules?** If so, sit down and work out a plan that everyone agrees on. Children can tell which parent is "softer" than the other. Agree to agree. United we stand!

- ⭐ **You have a difficult child?** Some children are more difficult than others (just as some adults are). The three main characteristics of difficult children are

    1. very strong emotions

    2. unpredictable behavior

    3. adapting to change slowly

Difficult children are challenging, but you can learn a lot from them. To handle them, do more of the same—keep up with the routine, but:

- ⭐ Be extra loving.

- ⭐ Be just as kind but firm. For example, say, "OK, let's pick up the toys now."

- ⭐ Make the routine longer and more involved. This makes your child feel secure because he knows what's coming next.

Tip ✶ ✶ ✶ ✶ ✶ ✶ ✶ ✶ ✶ ✶ ✶ ✶ ✶ ✶ ✶ ✶ ✶ ✶ ✶

🌙 Make sure your child gets lots of exercise and outdoor playtime. Take him for a brisk, afternoon walk or play in the yard, and he'll be more likely to be ready for bed.

Anna

Anna's parents couldn't to agree on her bedtime routine. Her father was like a drill sergeant and expected everything to be done in the right order, at the right time. He would yell if everything didn't go just as planned. Anna's mother was an easygoing person and enjoyed changing the routine.

Anna's parents always argued when Anna wanted to stay up late, or if she was being difficult about the bedtime routine. They tried not to argue in front of Anna, but it was hard. Anna's older brother would often join in when they argued—soon everyone in the family was upset.

Eventually, the parents called the doctor for help. The doctor said Anna would benefit from a regular bedtime routine. Once Anna was used to her routine, they would be able to change it once in a while without a problem. Trying this worked well, but the parents found they still had disagreements. They decided Anna's father felt most strongly about it, so he took over the bedtime routine.

How to Cope with the Uncooperative Child

You've tried to start a bedtime routine but your child doesn't want to cooperate. He won't turn off the television. He won't put away his toys. He agitates other children and pets. And he won't go to the bathroom. Take a deep breath to calm down, and try the following suggestions.

Won't turn off the television

Take out the plug or remove the fuse. Tell your child you won't turn it on the next day unless he lets you turn it off. Then encourage him to turn it off himself. He feels like he's on a team when you give him a job like this.

Won't put toys away

Don't put out so many toys the next night. You can also make a game out of it: "You collect all the blue ones and I'll find the red ones. Who can find the most?"

Agitates other children or your pets

"Divide and rule." In other words, separate them. Distract an older child with a puzzle while you get the younger one ready for bed. Put the pets in another room.

Won't go to the bathroom or get into the bath

Try the "running commentary" technique—for example, "Emily is going upstairs. She's on her way to the bathroom." If you're in the mood, use a rhyme or a limerick, like "Rub-a-dub-dub, three men in a tub . . ." It's silly, but it's fun and reduces tension. Your child is more likely to do what you want when you make it fun.

Won't undress

Try the counting method coupled with a challenge. "See if you can get your sweater off by the time I count to 5. Now see if you can take off your *shirt* by the time I get to 4." Or the running commentary: "Emily is taking off her sweater and now she's down to her shirt. . . ."

If your child is 4 or older, try to help him name each part of his clothing in Spanish (or any other language) such as *la camisa* for *shirt*. Even though your child may not know the right word, it's a distraction technique that will ease him into a routine. The following night, see if he can remember the Spanish words.

Bedtime

What time is bedtime? It's ironic that many an exhausted adult's idea of a good evening is to go to bed early. But a child's ideal evening is to go to bed as late as possible.

When they get older, this becomes a competition. "Jill's parents let her stay up until 8:30. Why can't I?" Even though right now your child is too young to swap bedtime notes with friends, it won't be long before he does! Be firm about bedtime from the beginning and it will help you in the long run.

A concrete bedtime for your child will help you both achieve independence. Plan time for yourself and for your partner. A child learns to respect boundaries when he knows that when the long hand reaches 12 and the short hand reaches 8, it's time for bed.

You can also use bedtimes to make him feel grownup. When an 8-year-old knows he goes to bed 30 minutes later than his 6-year-old sister, he feels more mature and is more likely to act accordingly. The actual time depends on your routine. If you have to pick up your 8-year-old from Cub Scouts at 8 P.M. on Tuesday evenings, it wouldn't work to set a bedtime of 8:30 P.M. for your 6-year-old, because it doesn't give you enough time to get home and go through your routine.

Set a time that helps you follow the routine in a relaxed way.

Similarly, if you need to pick up your husband from the train station at 6 P.M., you'll be rushed to start your 8-month-old's bedtime routine at 6:30 P.M. Set a time that helps you follow the routine in a relaxed way.

Bedtimes

As a rough rule of thumb, the following bedtimes are recommended:

Under	*before*
3 years old	7:30 P.M.
5 years old	8:00 P.M.
7 years old	8:30 P.M.
10 years old	9:00 P.M.
13 years old	9:30 P.M.
15 years old	10:00 P.M.

If your toddler still has a daytime nap, you may need to make bedtime later. But don't make it so late it gets dangerously close to your own bedtime. Move his morning nap forward. Encourage your toddler to go to sleep just before or after lunch. (Also see chapter 9.) Keep the nap short and gently wake him after 20 minutes so he has enough time to feel sleepy again before bedtime. Afternoon physical exercise, like taking a walk or playing in the yard, also helps wear out children so they're ready for bed.

Finally, remember that a good bedtime routine is like giving your child a present for life. You're helping him establish his independence in a loving and firm way. You're also helping him grow. We all need sleep to refresh our bodies and our minds. Think how bad you feel when you haven't spent enough time in bed. And then think how wonderful you feel when you *have*. Wouldn't you like to help your child feel the same way? It is possible!

Paul

When Paul was 5 years old, he was really slow at bedtime. As soon as the word "bed" was mentioned, he would slow down. He would finish his supper slowly, drag his feet going upstairs, and take forever to wash and get undressed.

His parents were patient. They thought it was important for Paul to express his personality. But the older he grew, the slower he became. His parents became progressively more annoyed. Then Grandma came to stay for a few nights. She was surprised at Paul's behavior because he was normal and active during the day. She devised games to help Paul speed up on his way to bed.

Each game worked for 1 or 2 nights and then Paul's parents would have to use something else. The games they played included "piggyback up the stairs," counting and expecting Paul to be in the bath by the count of 3, and then chasing him into the bath if he didn't make it in time. Other games included "the cold-water game"—if Paul didn't get out of the bath when he was asked, they would sprinkle cold water on him. Then there was "the monster-chasing game" and "the tickling game," which were threatened if he was too slow. Often the games would lead to hoots of laughter. In the end, Paul may not have gone to bed any quicker, but it was a lot more fun!

Routines

A routine only works if you persist and stick to it until it is well established. This may take about 6 months. But the benefits last for years. It may seem boring, exhausting and restrictive at times, but it has the following advantages:

✧ Fewer hassles at bedtime

✧ A more predictable child

✧ A flexible routine

✧ Your child will fall asleep faster

Your child's bedtime routine needs to be planned with the rest of the family in mind. It is helpful to write down the routine to clarify it for yourself and your partner. Following are a couple of examples of bedtime routines:

Sample Bedtime Routines

Steve, 11 months

4:30	Supper
5:00	Quiet play with toys
5:30	Put away toys. Steve helps by placing some of his blocks into a shape-sorting toy.
5:45	Steve's mother runs his bath and undresses him.
6:00	Bath time over—Steve's mother dries him and sings a counting song: "1, 2, 3, 4, 5." At the same time, she dries each relevant toe and finger before dressing Steve in his pajamas.
6:15	She dims the light and closes the curtains.
6:30	Steve's mother tucks him in bed, gives him his teddy bear.
6:40	She says a prayer or nursery rhyme with him, with actions. "God Bless Steve" (she points to Steve), "Mommy" (she points to herself), and so on.
6:50	Steve's mother turns out the light, goes out and shuts the door.

Amy, 2, and Tim, 9 months

5:00	Supper
5:30	Quiet play with toys. Amy helps her father put away the toys. He helps her read the clock and says it's 5:30 P.M. He takes her and Tim upstairs.

Continued . . .

5:45   Bath time. Amy's father helps Amy put toy ducks in the bath. When she splashes around too much, he tells her to "shhhhh" because it's nearly time for the ducks to go to bed. He bathes Tim at the same time.

6:00   Amy's father dries Tim in the bathroom and puts him in his baby seat while he dries Amy and puts her in her pajamas. They look at the clock on the bedroom wall. She can't tell the time yet but he points out the paper marker, which he has stuck on the clock. Amy can see the little hand is on the 6 and the big hand is on the 12. She knows that this is bedtime.

6:05   Amy's father reads her a story while she sits up in bed. He carries Tim into the room in his baby seat so he can watch him at the same time.

6:15   He hands Amy her special bedtime bear, "Reggie," who lives at the end of the bed.

6:20   Amy's father kisses her and says, "Goodnight, sleep tight." This is their special phrase. He goes out of the room and leaves the door slightly ajar. Amy doesn't like it completely shut.

6:25   Tim's dad reads him a short nursery rhyme and gives him his special bedtime security blanket.

6:30   He puts him in his crib, says, "Goodnight, sleep tight" and goes out of the room, shutting the door. (Tim hasn't learned to be afraid of the dark.)

At first, Amy's routine didn't go well.

7:00   Amy came into the kitchen. Her father was cooking supper. He said "Bedtime" and walked her back to her room, holding her in front of him but without cuddling her. He knew there was nothing wrong with her.

7:15   Amy came into the kitchen again. Her father did exactly the same as he did before. But he looked her in the eye and sounded very firm.

7:15   Amy cried in her bed. Her father sat on the steps outside, where she could see him.

7:35   Amy continued to cry. Her father sat outside the room but positioned so she couldn't see him.

7:55   Amy stopped crying.

8:00   Amy's father peeped in at the door. The bed was positioned in such a way that he could see her easily. She was fast asleep. He went downstairs.

After 6 days, Amy settled into a calmer routine. Although she didn't go to sleep immediately, she stopped coming out of the room because she knew she'd be returned to bed.

3

Keeping Your Child in His Crib or Bed

K eeping your baby in his crib shouldn't be a problem—after all, it has four sides! He shouldn't be able to get out until he's between 15 months and 2 years old. If your child is tall or a good climber, it might be sooner.

The longer you can keep your child in his crib, the better. It's like strapping him into a stroller or highchair—you know he's safe. The four crib sides create an important psychological barrier. They are the first example of a "psychological lock," like the bedroom door.

However, at some point your child will be able to climb over the side. This can be dangerous, obviously. If he escapes, try the following:

☆ Lower the side bar.

☆ Put a mattress beside the crib to cushion him if he falls.

☆ Make sure he is safe in *and* out of his room.

☆ Buy him a bed.

Lee

Lee's parents had worked hard to establish his bedtime routine. By the time he was 3 years old, Lee really enjoyed getting ready for bed. His problem was not

41

getting ready for bed—it started as soon as his parents said goodnight, turned off the light and left the room. Lee would immediately jump out of bed to see what his parents were doing. This had become part of his routine.

Lee's parents had recently taken him out of a crib and put him in a bed. This seemed to cause the trouble, so they put him back in the crib—even though he was getting too large for it. This worked well, except Lee enjoyed jumping up and down as if he were doing "crib aerobics." Their doctor told them it was normal. However, because Lee was growing, they were concerned he might climb out of his crib and fall on the floor. The doctor suggested putting a mattress, cushions or several layers of blankets on the floor to break Lee's fall.

Sure enough, in 6 weeks there was a loud crash in the middle of the night followed by Lee's screams. Fortunately, he didn't even have a bruise. But, Lee's parents were not going to risk another fall: They decided to leave him in the crib but leave the side down. After 2 weeks they transferred him to an ordinary bed. By then Lee was used to sleeping in a crib with no sides and not getting out, so he made no effort to get out of the bed.

Going from Crib to Bed

Many parents worry when their toddler progresses from a crib to a bed. One worry is that there won't be a physical barrier to stop him from getting out of bed. Encourage him to stay put and

- ✧ Be firm and consistent. As soon as you catch him getting out, say, "No. Back to bed!" in a firm, meaningful way. And put him back into bed.

- ✧ Choose a bed design with slightly raised, solid sides to discourage him from falling over the edge when he's asleep. The sides also make it more difficult for him to jump in and out of bed.

✄ Present the bed idea as another step up the "growing-up ladder." Tell your child he is such a good, grown-up boy that he is going to have his own bed. Isn't that wonderful? Make it fun and choose a new bedspread. Rearrange the room so it's a novelty to go to bed—and stay there.

✄ Buy a bed guard that conforms to U.S. and Canadian safety standards. (See the appendix for more information.) Make sure your child's head can't get trapped between the slats.

✄ Think carefully about the pros and cons of bunk beds if you are considering them. These may be more suitable when your child is 5 or older and used to staying in bed. Some children are scared of the top bunk and can fall out. Others don't like to be closed in on the bottom bunk.

Stick with It!

Now comes the tricky part. If your child jumps out of bed or screams the minute you turn your back, it's tempting to pick him up and take him with you as you finish your dinner or deal with the other kids—but be strong! You are teaching him independence and self-control. Later in life he will be happy with his own company and will have inner security and self-confidence.

Safety, Again

Check to be sure your child's room is still safe. We can't emphasize enough how important this is. Has your child opened a closet door or pulled out his toys since you put him to bed. No? Then there's no reason not to put him back into his safe environment and expect him to stay there.

Your Child's Health

Is your child sick? Always consider this when your child is upset at night. Does he have a temperature? Is he hot? Does he have a rash? Has he been sick?

Sick children tend to be quieter than normal, although they may also be more demanding. It can be difficult to tell when a child is ill. Use a thermometer to help determine whether your child has a fever. Always check with your family doctor if you are not sure if your child is sick.

If your child is healthy and his room is safe, it's reasonable to expect him to stay in his room. Sound difficult? Think about how you walk down the street with your child. Are you confident about his safety? Are you sure he won't run into the street? If you are sure, how did you accomplish it? You probably taught him by warning him repeatedly how dangerous the street was.

Use the same psychological approach to keep your child in his room. Obviously a truck isn't going to run over your child if he walks out of his room, but tell yourself it's just as important he stay put at night. Your conviction will rub off on him. It is important. It's a vital step toward his independence and growth.

If your child has not learned to stay safely on the sidewalk, you need more practice. Encouraging your child to stay in his room and stay on the sidewalk are both examples of how you can help your child learn to control himself. The only way children learn self-control is by being controlled from the outside first.

"Training" and "routine" are the key words. Get him into a bedtime routine as soon as you can. Train your child and reward him with praise. (See the section on Rewards, page 109.)

Leaving Your Child Alone

Being alone does not cause psychological harm. Children who do *not* learn to be alone can end up with problems. You help your child learn how to be alone and how to develop self-control by leaving him alone in his bedroom. He discovers he does not need to be with you all the time in order to be safe. If he controls his urge to be comforted by others, he will be able to comfort himself, and feel safe and secure during the night.

Learning to be alone is a gradual process, which continues throughout a child's life. It's best if parents take the first steps to control the process early, when they know their child is absolutely safe. This book provides an excellent opportunity to help your child take his first steps toward self-confidence and inner security.

Baby's Cries

When a baby cries, it's natural for parents to respond by picking him up, cuddling or feeding him. Crying awakens powerful emotions in parents. You want to protect your children—it's only natural.

Never ignore a newborn baby's cries. Most parents would find it impossible anyway. When you're still getting to know your baby, you're not sure exactly why he is crying. Until you are confident and know your baby better, you won't be able to relax. The following checklist helps you rule out some common reasons babies cry and find out why *your* baby is crying:

- Is he hungry?

- Is he damp?

- Is he too hot or too cold?

- Is he ill?

- Is he in pain?

How to Tell Why Your Baby Is Crying

If your baby stops crying as soon as you pick him up, probably nothing is wrong. If you're not sure, try to put him down. If he cries, pick him up again to see what happens. If he stops again, you can be pretty sure it's not too serious.

If your baby continues to cry, do the following:

- Hold your baby against your shoulder and sway from side to side, patting his back very gently. Rock him in a baby-carrier. Swaying movements put children to sleep. Best of all, put him in a baby sling strapped to your body and rock him to sleep that way.

- Sing gently. Lullabies are a wonderful invention! Many adults still can remember the lullabies their mothers sang to them and pass them on to their own children. The soft sound of a familiar parent's voice is often enough to lull your child to sleep.

- Use other sounds. Turn on the vacuum cleaner. The low hum often reassures a baby. Even better, make your own low humming noise instead of relying on a machine. Some parents use a "white music" tape, sounds of rain falling or brooks babbling. Any repetitive sound, such as a ticking clock, a vacuum cleaner or a washing machine, has a soothing effect.

But, your baby might become hooked on these sounds and movements and won't settle down until you have gone through a whole performance! To avoid this, watch for the first signs of drowsiness and drooping eyelids. Then put your baby in the crib right away instead of continuing to hold him. Continue the sounds and movements as you put him down. If your baby starts to cry almost immediately, keep humming, but don't pick him up. Change the sound as little as possible. If your baby figures out he can't change his small world by crying, he might get bored and give up.

When your brand-new baby cries, you stop what you're doing and turn to him immediately. When he's a few weeks or months old, you might finish your conversation first. You'll know your child well before you let him cry. It's almost an art form to know when to jump in. Expect to get a lot of practice—your under-6-month-old baby is bound to wake up crying, at least once in a while!

Older Babies and Toddlers

There comes a point when you have to stop comforting your baby to get him to sleep. Will you still be standing there, crooning to your 8-year-old, and if so, what will you be doing when he is 18? It's unlikely. You have to find a way of phasing it out.

Now comes the difficult part—you've put your older baby or toddler into his crib and he objects by yelling or trying to get out. Before you rush in, remember the crib has sides. It is not a problem to leave him in the crib if you know he is safe and OK. If you've checked on him and gone through the calming routine, then it is *all right* to let him cry. The thorny question of whether to let him cry, is such a big issue that it needs its own chapter (see the following chapter).

In and Out of Bed

Here's what to do if your child "escapes" from bed:

☆ Catch him as quickly as you can—before your child gets out of his room. If he sees exciting things happening in the rest of the house, he'll be even more reluctant to do a U-turn. You're in charge! So take him back to bed.

☆ Use simple words. Don't try to reason. You're an adult and you don't need to justify your actions. (That's one of the few perks in parenting!) Use phrases like, "You'll be tired in the morning," "I need to cook supper" or a simple "Back to bed." These phrases leave little room for argument—and even a 15-month-old can do that!

☆ *Look* firm. Are you saying "no" with a sympathetic look? Then it's not surprising your child is getting mixed messages. Make sure you *look* like you mean what you are saying. Everyone has a special look that says, "I have had enough of this. I am really serious now!" If you don't think you have this look, ask your partner. It would be surprising if you have never used it on him or her.

☆ Sound firm—you don't have to be a dragon but you do have to be determined. Simply utter the word "bed" with conviction. You mean it—you have to make sure *he* knows you mean it. It helps to put extra emphasis on the beginning and end of words.

☆ Use firm gestures—back up what you say with a definite and clear gesture. Let there be no confusion. Point clearly to the bed, just like the simple gestures police use to direct traffic. They are so clear and firm that no one dares ignore them.

Danielle

Danielle was an easy baby. As she grew older she was well behaved—until she was 3 years old and was admitted to the hospital with a chest infection. It disturbed her. When she returned home she woke up during the night and cried for her parents. They weren't surprised by her reaction. They did everything they could to reassure her and responded quickly to her cries. If they didn't go into her room immediately, Danielle would get out of bed and go into their room.

After a few months she stopped crying, but she continued to wake up and go into her parents' room. By the age of 4½, Danielle was regularly getting up during the night and getting into bed on her father's side. She had figured out he was less likely to take her back to bed than her mother was. After several more months of disturbed nights, her parents decided to do something about it. Because Danielle's mother was more able to be firm, they decided she would be the one to take Danielle back to her room.

They rearranged the furniture so it was impossible for Danielle to get around to her father's side of the bed without waking both of them. Danielle's mother discovered Danielle would go back to bed easily if she held her firmly and marched her to bed saying sharply, "Go back to bed immediately." She would keep a serious and determined look on her face. Then Danielle's mother said the usual goodnight phrase, which helped Danielle fall asleep quickly.

Danielle's father was resentful his wife was more effective at this than he was. Because he felt she was too strict, he tried to compensate by being softer and more easygoing. They realized their different styles of discipline caused problems during the day. The father agreed to be firmer. His wife taught him to use his facial expression, his gesture and his voice to make it clear to Danielle he meant what he said.

This worked and he realized it was better to act like a firm father than to be taken advantage of by his 4-year-old daughter. Now she paid attention to him. He no longer had to repeat himself until he lost his temper, which made Danielle stop whatever she was doing to look at her father as if to say, "Why are you getting so worked up?"

Act Convincing

Put on a performance to get your way. Pretend you're an actor. Your toddler is the audience. Play the part! Make your gestures dramatic: "BED!" If your child is not impressed, your perfor-

> If your child is not impressed, your performance is not good enough.

mance is not good enough. Try again or ask your partner or a friend to do it for you. Learn from them. Can you pick up any acting tips? You may have to put on an award-winning performance to impress your young audience.

Bedtime is one of the most difficult times because you're tired at the end of the day. You're less patient. The smallest thing can annoy you. Acting can be relaxing. You can say to yourself, "This is not really me—it is only an act. Let's see if I can impress the audience tonight!"

Pretend your child who won't go to bed isn't really yours. Sounds strange? Think about it. What if you were watching a friend's child for the night, and *he* wouldn't go back to bed. Would you scream at him? Probably not. You'd try to be firm in a kind way. Do the same with your own child.

Avoid the word "please." It's surprisingly easy to beg your child to do what you're telling him. And that would be giving him the wrong message. You're in charge. Remember?

Back to Bed

Your child is quick—before you know it, he's out of his room and down the hall. *Don't* chase him. Get him back to his room with as little attention as possible. If you run after him, you're giving him plenty of attention. He might enjoy the chase! Don't say anything—just walk up to him calmly. And then catch him.

- Resist the temptation to talk to him. Again, the less attention you give him the better. He's not really there . . .

- Don't look at him. He should be in bed, not running around. If you pay as little attention to him as possible, he may decide it's not worth his while to get up all the time.

- Walk him back, in front of you. Don't pick him up for a hug. Why should he go back to bed if he can stay up with you instead? If you walk with him just in front of you, he'll know you mean business.

✧ Use a firm hold. How you hold your child sends a clear message. A gentle hug means "I'm enjoying this." A firm hold means "I mean what I say." An uncomfortable hold means "I'm completely fed up." There is no need to cause any pain. This only increases the crying and delays sleep. Your hold tells him how determined you are.

✧ Take him back to bed, say "goodnight" firmly, using the special words, and walk out of the room. If he gets out of bed again, walk him back using the steps already described. Keep going. It's tiring. It's boring. It consumes your time. There are so many other things you could be doing instead—like cleaning up or simply relaxing with your partner. *But when you succeed*, you have earned future evenings of free time to do what you want.

By taking your child back to bed calmly every time, either you or your child will eventually give up. You have to make sure *he's* the one to give up and not you. *Decide* to succeed. All you have to do is keep going. It may take 3 evenings or more. Soon your child will no longer jump out of bed.

Why Be Firm?

Children need to know their limits—what they can do and what they can't do. Firm, clear guidelines keep children safe. When you teach your child to avoid dangers such as fire, electricity, water and heights, you cannot afford to be half-hearted about it. It is not something to negotiate or explain with detailed answers. You have to be absolutely firm and clear with your child to teach him not to put his fingers in the electric socket or run into the street. It is a matter of life and death.

This book provides an opportunity for you to practice being firm in a situation where it is not a matter of life and death. Practice being firm about bedtime and about your child staying in bed. If it doesn't work, no harm is done and all you need is to practice a little more. When you achieve your goal you will know your child is safer than before.

Every time you say goodnight, he'll realize it isn't worth it to resist. When you are truly determined, your child learns to do what you say and understands you really do mean it! (For example, he stays in his room with the door open and doesn't leave because he knows you mean business.) When that happens, give yourself a pat on the back. You've succeeded in putting a "psychological lock" on your child's bedroom door. The benefit of a "psychological lock" is your child has learned not to leave the room unless he has your permission.

> Train your child to keep within the boundaries and praise him when he does so.

After you've given yourself a pat on the back, praise your child too. Remember the phrase "positive training." Train your child to keep within the boundaries and praise him when he does so. Tell him how pleased you are when he stays in bed. If he's old enough, reward him for good behavior.

Thomas

Thomas learned to sleep in an ordinary bed when he was 3 years old. By 4 years old, he was active and started to get out of bed at night to roam around the house. This was all right before his parents went to bed because they heard him creeping around and were able to take him straight back to bed. It was different during the night because they were both deep sleepers.

Sometimes they would wake to find Thomas sitting downstairs in front of the television at 3 A.M. They wondered whether he had been sleepwalking. The doctor told them it was unlikely because sleepwalkers only carry out very simple tasks and usually stay deep asleep. Thomas' parents were worried he might get hurt as he wandered around in the middle of the night. They put a gate in his doorway, which worked until he learned to climb over it.

His parents decided to install a burglar alarm with an infrared movement detector to cover the stairs and part of the hall. They explained to Thomas what they had done,

*but he didn't pay attention until he heard the alarm go off
when he came out of his room in the middle of the night.
Thomas was so shocked, he never tried it again!*

Common Questions and Issues

"My child starts crying when I leave him alone in his room."

It sounds harsh. But if you want your child to establish a good
sleep pattern, you have to help him learn that crying will not
bring you back. He has to learn that when he goes to bed, he goes
to sleep. He's not there to play the "trap the parent" game.
(Extra points are awarded for speed of arrival and the length of
time a parent stays. The child gets a bonus point if the parent
brings a drink.)

Perhaps your child is lonely. When you come in and pick him
up when he cries, he learns what to do. He'll cry the next night
and the night after—so you will come in again and again. As a
result, he won't learn how to go to sleep on his own. He'll always
need you.

"My child is afraid of the dark."

If you start early enough, there's no reason for this fear. After
all, your baby was in the womb for 9 months without electric
lights. Of course, complete darkness makes it difficult to check
on your baby and for your older child to find the bathroom. But
keep the light on *outside* the bedroom and under *your* control.

Look at it another way—by leaving the light on you say "dark
is dangerous" to your child. A fear of the dark is natural.
Everyone has to be careful in the dark. It's easy to bump into
things or trip over them, but the dark is not dangerous.

It is a basic instinct to be afraid of the dark. In earlier times, it
was dangerous to go out at night and risk being hurt by wild animals. But this does not happen in the bedroom which, by now,
you've made sure is totally safe. Children need to know they are
safe in their beds at night in the dark. The only way they can
learn this is by sleeping in a dark room.

The Dark Is Not Dangerous

If your child is safely tucked in bed then the dark is not dangerous. Only when children wander around in the dark can they trip over something or bump into furniture. That is one reason to make sure your child's room is totally safe.

Children who learn to cope in the dark have gained another skill and will be all the more confident for it. People who are blind do not get anxious because their world is dark. In fact, they gain other coping skills and abilities most of us don't have. The ideas in this book help children become confident in the dark. As a result, they gain extra coping skills.

Sadly, even many adults are not happy about being in the dark at night because they were afraid of the dark as children. So, if your child is still a baby, begin instilling confidence early on.

If you don't start this routine until later and your child has already developed a fear of the dark, wean him off this fear by using an electric plug-in nightlight or leave the hall light on. Another idea is to use lower-watt bulbs or any other safe way of shielding light from your child.

Tip · ★ · ★ · ★ · ★ · ★ · ★ · ★ · ★ · ★ · ★ · ★ · ★ · ★ · ★

Pretend, with your toddler, that his bed is like a ship. It's a safe place to be. Close your eyes—you can almost hear the sea . . .

As your child gets more used to going to bed, start leaving lights off or use a dimmer switch. The idea is to encourage him to feel comfortable without providing extra help. It's yet another step on his climb to independence and self-confidence.

There's also a fascinating chemical fact about darkness. Your child's pineal gland (an endocrine organ that helps regulate biorhythms)—and yours too—naturally produces the substance *melatonin*. Melatonin is a natural sedative that automatically quiets the body in preparation for sleep. The release of melatonin is stimulated by darkness. By encouraging your child to accept the dark, you do him a favor. You're also encouraging the production of melatonin, which makes him want to rest and relax his body.

"My child will only sleep in my bed."

Some research shows that SIDS, sudden infant death syndrome, or crib death, is less likely to occur if young babies sleep in a parent's bedroom during the first few weeks or months. (See page 106 for more information on SIDS.) However, this can lead to problems if it continues too long. Research also shows that parents and children who share the same room or bed both wake up more. So neither of you gets the rest you need.

Toddlers and even older babies can learn to dislike bedtime so much they will only go to sleep in Mommy and Daddy's bed. Sometimes we're to blame for this. If your child won't stay in bed, it's tempting to lie down with him—if only to shut your own tired eyes after a hard day! It's also tempting to do this on your own bed, which is probably bigger and more comfortable. Your baby, and most certainly your toddler, gets used to this. It's nice to have someone lying next to you. You know that yourself if you are in a steady, happy relationship with a cozy double bed.

> Research also shows that parents and children who share the same room or bed both wake up more.

If you don't mind the idea of your child being in your bed for the next four years, that's up to you. But if you do, then do something about it fast, before the habit sticks! Ask yourself who makes the rules in your family. Do you, or does your child have the final say?

Some parents lie down with their child, wait until he's asleep and then gently carry him to his own bed. The obvious disadvantage is that when your child wakes up at night and realizes you are no longer there, he's more likely to come and find you! If he's used to going to sleep on his own, he'll probably turn over and go back to sleep again.

It's also tempting to let your child doze off in front of the television after the bath-time routine. Again, this is an adult habit more than a child's! It has short-term benefits. You can *watch* your favorite program instead of sitting with your child in his room and only hearing the theme music. And you aren't missing precious evening time with your partner. But the drawback is, your child gets used to it. Why would he want to go to bed after his bath when he's used to staying with you?

At some point, your child has to learn to go to bed on his own. The longer you delay that day, the harder it is for both of you to break the habit.

"My child won't let me leave him—he cries and screams every time."

Who is in charge? If *you* are in charge, you can teach your child not to cry any more.

Start by teaching yourself the difference in your child's various cries. You can learn to distinguish among cries that signal

✧ Real distress

✧ Anger

✧ Attention-seeking demands

✧ Teething

✧ Automatic habit

Do this by listening carefully to the cries he makes in different situations. It's like cracking a secret code. Children cry for a number of reasons.

Pain or discomfort

The cause may be obvious—but if not, seek professional advice.

Separation anxiety

Remember, this is normal and natural. Get your child used to being separated from you for short periods during the day. Do it gradually. Start by leaving the room for a short time. This can be extended into short trips out, away from your child, so you both get used to being without each other. Gradual daytime separations help your child become used to being separated from you at night.

Anger

Ask yourself what your child is angry about. Is it reasonable or is it an automatic habit because you're not there? Check by going into his room. If he stops crying, your child is more likely to be manipulating you. But if the crying continues when you're there, he's more likely to be crying because of real distress, not just anxiety or anger.

Pablo

Pablo cried a lot as a baby but his parents persevered and eventually they were able to settle him into a good sleep routine when he was 18 months old. All went well until he was 2½ years old. Then, for no apparent reason, he refused to go to bed at night and would wake up at night, crying for Mommy. The parents went through a checklist of what could be wrong with Pablo. Was he ill? Was it teething, colic, pain, discomfort, loneliness, a nightmare? It wasn't clear.

They noticed Pablo had become more clingy during the day and it was difficult to leave him alone for more than a few moments. He cried every time they took him to daycare and screamed when they left. The doctor suggested Pablo might have separation anxiety. It normally develops between 6 and 8 months old and can become a problem at 18 months old.

The doctor suggested Pablo experience happy separations. This meant teaching him he could handle being on his own by leaving him for progressively longer periods of time. During the day, they left Pablo with a friend for a few minutes before returning. They gradually increased the time spent apart from their son. At night, the parents did the same—by leaving Pablo in bed longer and longer before returning full of praise and encouragement.

Relieving Separation Anxiety

Wean your child from your attention either rapidly or gradually.

Rapid—Let your child cry (see also chapter 4). You've already checked him, so you know nothing is wrong.

Gradual—Stay in the room with your child and gradually decrease the amount of time you spend there. For examples, see page 77.

Tip . ★ . ★ . ★ . ★ . ★ . ★ . ★ . ★ . ★ . ★ . ★ . ★ . ★ . ★ . ★

Give older toddlers a simple, practical reason why you
have to leave the room. Explain that you need to turn
off the stove. Your child might accept a practical reason
for your departure.

Lisa

*Lisa was 3 years old and really enjoyed being read to last
thing at night. The only problem was the longer the story,
the more likely she was to wake up at night. After
discussing the problem with friends, Lisa's parents
realized this was not unusual and that toddlers don't sleep
as well if they have spent a long time with the parent
before going to sleep. The older Lisa became, the more
demanding she was. Her parents had to read a whole
book before she would allow them to stop.*

*Although Lisa's parents wanted her to learn as much as
possible from reading, they decided they would have to
limit her to 5 minutes. They explained this to Lisa and
used a cooking timer to "ping" when the time was up.
They offered to read at a normal speed or they could read
at a very fast speed and finish the book in 5 minutes.
After hearing her father read quickly and not being able
to understand any of it, Lisa opted for the ordinary
reading rate for the 5 minutes. Her parents were
surprised at how well she accepted this.*

Common Questions and Issues

"I usually spend about 20 minutes with my child at night before going out of the room. Is that too long?"
Ask yourself if the problem lies with you. Are you lonely? Is your partner out or not there at all? If so, perhaps it's time to develop some independence for yourself. Alternatively, are you afraid of something? If so, what? Your child is healthy and his bedroom is safe. Think about your child. He needs time alone to rest and grow. Help him by giving him that time.

"I don't have time to keep taking my child back to his bed."
Of course you don't! Not many parents do. You have other children to look after. You need to clean up the house. And you're exhausted.

Make the rest of your life as simple as possible. Prepare a simple dinner in advance because you know you won't have much time to spend in the kitchen. Keep your other children occupied with books, games or a suitable video if necessary. Let the house stay messy for a few evenings until your child is into his new routine. It's only for a short time. When you've succeeded, you'll have your evenings back again. But if you give up, you'll lose those precious evenings for several years to come.

If you are a single parent, it can be really difficult. Do you have a friend or relative who could help you? If two of you are at home, take turns running the bedtime routine. Better still, do it together.

Two parents putting on an act of total determination is usually very impressive. If it isn't, you may have more serious problems ahead. How will you control your child in dangerous situations? Perhaps you both need some acting lessons to improve your performance. If one of your friends seems to be able to make an impression on children, ask him or her for tips.

"My partner comes home just when I've put my child to bed."
It's not surprising the sound of the key turning in the lock or the doorbell makes your toddler leap out of bed to see Mommy or Daddy. Work out a plan with your partner. Perhaps it's best if he

comes in quietly and doesn't see his son. Sound tough? The alternative is to say goodnight briefly and then pay for it by your child wanting to be up all evening. Wouldn't it be better for your child to have a good night's sleep and then give your partner more quality time, maybe alone, with your child on the weekend?

Alternatively, you might prefer to follow the usual bedtime wind-down ritual until you hear your partner returning. Don't get as far as saying goodnight to your child. Get your partner to calmly finish off the routine. Then he or she can say goodnight and leave the room.

The disadvantage is that this brief appearance might not be enough. Your child might want to see more of Mommy or Daddy who has been out all day. So if it doesn't work, your partner may have to take over the bedtime routine on weekends when he or she is home.

"What if my child is sick?"

Clearly, the routine may have to change if your child is sick. When he dozes off during the day he won't want to sleep at night. The bedtime routine can be very reassuring for a sick child. Even though your child may not feel well, at least the routine is familiar and predictable.

As we've explained, going to bed doesn't necessarily mean going to sleep. It can also mean resting. If your sick toddler is awake at 8 P.M. and really can't sleep because he had a nap at 6 P.M., don't worry. The rest will do him good. You may need to check more often to see what you can do to make him more comfortable.

Sick children need lots of extra love and attention. But as soon as your child starts to get better, go back to your original routine. Don't wait until he's fully recovered, because the longer the gap, the more difficult it is to return to the normal routine.

"My child is too tired to sleep."

It's true that some children get to a stage where they're overtired. They're beyond sleep. They're exhausted and irritable! They may throw temper tantrums. They're beyond reason. Even normal tactics don't pacify them.

Tired children become hyperactive and disobedient. Bedtime routine is particularly helpful for a child who is overtired. Once the routine is established, a tired child will follow it automatically. In any case, it is not the sleep that is most important. The goal is for your child to stay quietly in bed. Sleep will come—eventually.

The Hyperactive Child

It's often difficult getting any child to bed. But if your child is hyperactive, it can be even harder. The key is to remember these children lack self-control. They are often smart, but usually they are somewhat immature and need extra control from the outside.

Help by controlling your child in a kind but firm way. To help a hyperactive child go to bed—even if it's to rest rather than to sleep—just do *more* of the same. In other words, do what we've already advised, but do more of it.

- Give more routine. Do things in the same order as you draw closer to bedtime. Let it become a hypnotic, reassuring sequence of events that comforts him.

- Be consistent. Do what you say you'll do. Don't do one thing one evening and something else another evening.

- Be kind but firm.

Joey

Joey was a very active, restless child. As he grew older and mixed with other children it was obvious he had less self-control than other children did. He was clumsy and could not concentrate for long. He didn't sleep well but never woke up his parents at night. He either played quietly in bed or roamed around his room. If he did sleep through the night, the sheets were a mess in the morning.

When Joey was 5 years old and started school, his teacher complained about his overactivity. Joey was disruptive. A doctor referred the boy to a child psychiatrist, who diagnosed Attention Deficit and Hyperactivity Disorder (ADHD).

The doctor told Joey's parents that this condition occurred more commonly in boys and tended to run in families. The main cause was developmental immaturity, which affected the ability to have self-control. The parents were given exercises for Joey that provided more external control for him at first and then taught him how to control himself for increasingly longer periods of time.

They were told diet was unlikely to be a cause of Joey's hyperactivity—though the control involved in going on a diet seemed to help some children. Joey's parents asked about drugs for ADHD and were told a number of drugs were available that dealt only with the symptoms of the disorder and were not usually prescribed under the age of 7.

Joey had to learn to control his attention and his impulses by himself. There was a good chance that hard work at this stage would help him grow out of the problem.

Over the next year Joey's parents and teacher worked hard to help him, and gradually his behavior improved. His parents were happy to see Joey gain more self-control, as well as improved sleep patterns.

Common Questions and Issues

"There's so much noise in the house that my child wants to see what's going on."

You can't stop the other children from talking or stop the phone from ringing because your child needs to go to sleep. Resist the temptation to creep quietly around the house. Your child needs to get used to normal sounds of life around him. The sooner you start, the sooner he'll get used to it.

"I have problems in my personal life, and I think my children are picking up on that."

Children are adept at discovering secrets, especially if they're secrets you'd rather they didn't know. Children also pick up on emotional disturbances in the home. This can interfere with their sleep. It is only natural that if you are close to your child, he will pick up on your feelings. It is best to give a simple explanation that is as reassuring as possible.

We don't pretend there are easy answers. There aren't. But being a parent carries a responsibility. If you remember your own parents arguing or being upset over something, you'll know how much it hurt. As a parent, you are older and wiser than your children. It's up to you not to burden them with adult troubles. Find a quiet space or time to yourself where you can be upset without anyone seeing. Also, try to find a friend or relative who can support you through a difficult time.

"I feel so annoyed with my child that I want to spank him when he gets out of bed."

It's understandable. But don't! Spanking agitates you and your child. It disturbs your calm, measured "you're-going-back-to-bed" walk described earlier. So take a deep breath and repeat those steps instead. (See pages 49-50.)

Spanking is like taking out a bank loan. It may help in a crisis, but the cost is high because you have to pay it back with interest. The guilt you may feel after spanking can easily make you overindulgent next time your child is being difficult. (For more on spanking, see chapter 8.)

"I feel like giving up."

Don't! If at first you don't succeed, try, try again. As parents, set an example and help your children get through future difficulties by persevering even when things are difficult.

If you give up, your child learns it's all right to give up when the going gets tough. He also thinks you'll back down in other areas, such as schoolwork or dinnertime.

In a world where everything changes all the time and there is so much uncertainty, it is reassuring for children to know there can be continuity and predictability. It helps them feel secure.

"I can't reason with my child when I say he has to stay in bed."

Then don't! Children under the age of 8 have not reached the age of reason. Their system of logic is different than an adult's. Stick to practicalities and give simple explanations.

Alan

Alan was 4 years old and very bright. He always questioned his parents, asking them "Why…?". When he started asking his parents why he had to go to sleep, they usually had a response. At first he was satisfied by simple answers. Then one night, Alan decided he really wanted to know why he had to go to bed. His parents, who had always tried to answer Alan's questions, searched for an answer that would satisfy him. It took several hours to get him to his bedroom. By midnight Alan was drowsy but he wasn't persuaded by reason to go to sleep. His parents gave Alan reasons for 3 hours and were about to snap. Fortunately, Alan finally drifted off to sleep. His parents decided they would never reason with their son in the same way again. They had discovered what many parents do: Reasoning with a 4- or 5-year-old—or even a child who is a lot older—can be a waste of time. This is because young children's logic system differs greatly from adults'.

Fall-Back Method

Some children take longer to learn how to stay put in bed than others. Try the following fall-back method to help your child stay in his room. You may need to put a gate at the entrance to the room. If so, make sure your child won't start climbing over it in a bid for freedom. Obviously, this could be dangerous.

Also make sure the room is still safe. Check every now and then to see all is well. But don't socialize! Don't offer to read another story or play a game. It's bedtime. And as we've said earlier, going to bed doesn't necessarily mean going to sleep. It means resting, too.

Eventually, your child will give up. Before you know it, you'll look in and see he's fallen asleep. He might even be asleep on the floor. Wait 5 minutes to make sure he's really asleep and then move him into his warm bed.

If you can't do this without waking him up, put extra clothes on him, keep the room warm and let him sleep on the floor if that is where he is most comfortable.

Then kick back and give yourself a pat on the back again. Put a sticker on your own star chart! You've done it. But remember—you need to *keep doing it*. The next night. And the next. *And* the next. Until finally, you reach an evening when your child stays in bed on his own. Yes—one evening, this will happen! The more determined you are about it, the sooner that evening will come.

> Finally, you reach an evening when your child stays in bed on his own.

Letting Your
Child Cry

B y now, you can see that helping your child get a good night's
rest follows a natural progression. As your child grows from
baby to toddler and into an older child, your reaction to
each sleep stage affects the next.

You probably rocked or soothed him to sleep as a baby. When
he was a toddler, you might have battled to keep him in his room
even if he wasn't sleeping. Eventually, a time comes when every
parent decides that their child needs to sleep in his own bed for
the whole night.

What to Do When He Cries

You've reached the stage where your child stays in his room, but
still yells and cries for you. Remember: Crying is normal. It doesn't
necessarily mean something is seriously wrong. Adults have many
ways of expressing themselves, such as talking, singing and danc-
ing. But very young children only have one method: crying.

Often, crying does mean something is wrong, such as a wet
diaper, hunger or gas. So it's natural for parents to respond to crying babies. The sound almost gives parents a physical pain. It's
nature's way of prodding parents into checking that everything is
all right.

But as your children grow older, you can't continue to respond to them as you did when they were babies. Start to delay your response gradually. The time to start working on crying during the night is when the child is between 6 months and 1 year. After the age of 2 or 3, a good sleep habit is more difficult for a child to achieve. But it's still possible.

After the age of 5 it's even harder—but not impossible. In fact, some children don't sleep well until they are 5 because by then, they're in school. The physical exhaustion of a full school day makes them want to go to sleep and they need sleep to help them cope with their busy lives. But 5 years is a long time to wait for a good night's sleep!

Yes, You Can Let Your Child Cry

Imagine what would happen if you responded immediately *every* time your child cried. He would learn that whenever he wanted your attention or anything else, all he has to do is cry. We all have to learn to delay gratification. It is best for children to learn this before they go to school or are supervised by other adults. These adults will not respond immediately to your child's cries and demands for attention.

Giving your child a sleep program helps him learn that *you* make the rules and decisions about his well-being. It teaches your child to be confident that you make the right decisions on his behalf. He learns to trust you because he wakes up safe and sound in the morning.

Leaving a child alone to cry is OK. It is part of the sleep program. Believe it or not, leaving your child alone to cry in bed is a way to show your love and care for him. It helps him learn to manage his emotions and know he is safe and secure in your care even if his every demand for attention is not met.

Leaving Your Child Alone to Cry

Leaving your child alone to cry sounds heartless. But look at it this way: If you can help your child get himself to sleep, you'll be preparing him for a life of independence. If you stick to the Three-Day Sleep Plan that follows on pages 68 to 70, you'll have an 80% chance of seeing improvement!

Rebecca

Rebecca, a 3-year-old, hardly ever slept through the night. She and her younger brother, Richard, lived alone with their mother. Their parents were divorced. Their father took them out for the day every other weekend. Rebecca would often sleep with her mother and was restless. She refused to go to bed alone and insisted on staying up until her mother went to bed.

It was clear Rebecca was not getting enough sleep because she was restless, irritable and overactive during the day. Both their doctor and friends gave the same advice—Rebecca needed a bedtime routine and a fixed bedtime. She also needed to be in her own bed for at least 12 hours to get enough rest and sleep. Rebecca's mother had tried insisting—and then forcing—Rebecca to stay in her room at bedtime. However, Rebecca would cry and scream until her mother couldn't stand it any more.

On one occasion, when her mother had decided to be really tough, she let Rebecca scream for an hour and a half. Eventually Rebecca made herself sick. Her mother felt so guilty that she brought Rebecca into her bed. Rebecca was still not getting enough sleep or rest and continued to be demanding, irritable and hyperactive during the day. Her mother had no time for herself in the evening.

Eventually, she decided "enough was enough." After discussing the problem with a close friend, they agreed they would work on Rebecca's bad sleep habit together. They decided to try the Three-Day Sleep Plan. Before starting, Rebecca's mother and her friend made sure the bedroom was completely safe and Rebecca was well.

The friend agreed to look after Richard for a few nights while Rebecca was learning to sleep in her own bed. They worked out a bedtime routine and wrote it down, with the timing given for each stage. They also worked out what could possibly go wrong and agreed on a plan to deal with every potential problem. (See pages 69-70.) If all else failed, she would phone her friend any time during the night if she felt she were about to give in to Rebecca's screams.

They discussed whether or not this was a fair and reasonable thing to do for Rebecca and whether it would harm her. As it happened, the friend had been through a very similar situation with her own daughter, who was about the same age as Rebecca. She had screamed for 2 hours on the first night, for 1 hour the next night and hardly at all on the third night. She now stayed quietly in her room during the night and was better behaved during the day. This encouraged Rebecca's mother to follow the plan through to the end.

On the first night, Rebecca screamed for an hour and then threw up. Her mother came into the room, cleaned up the mess, made Rebecca comfortable with minimum fuss and then left the room. The screaming started again and occurred on and off during the next 2 hours.

Fortunately, the neighbors had been warned about what was happening that night, so their possible reaction was one less thing to worry about. At 4 A.M. Rebecca eventually fell asleep. When her friend called at 9 A.M. the next morning, Rebecca's mother told her she was never going to go through that again because she was completely exhausted. The friend suggested she try it one more night. She agreed. The next morning she woke up and realized Rebecca had slept through the night.

Rebecca continued to sleep through the nights thereafter. Her mother and her friend agreed it must have been the night Rebecca screamed so much that solved the problem. It was also surprising to note how much better behaved Rebecca was during the day. She was less irritable and seemed happier.

Three-Day Sleep Plan

Safety First

The Three-Day Sleep Plan can only be justified if your child is completely safe in his room and both physically and psychologically healthy. Here is the checklist:

✧ How was your child during the day?

✧ Was he in a bad mood or anxious?

✧ Has he had a temperature recently?

✧ Are there reasons why he might be upset?

✧ Have you double-checked the room for safety?

✧ Do you feel well and safe yourself?

You can go ahead with the rapid approach, the Three-Day Sleep Plan, with confidence when you know your child is healthy and feeling OK.

Demands for Attention

Bathroom or Drink Requests

If your child says he needs a drink or the bathroom, don't answer these calls. He's already been to the bathroom and had a drink. If he comes out of his room to ask again, tell him in a few short words that he took care of those needs. Take him back to bed. (See chapter 3.)

Bed Wetting

If he tells you he's wet the bed, ignore him. You can clean it up in the morning. Thousands of children wet the bed or their diaper every night and do not get cleaned up until morning. If this is a continual problem, put extra layers on the bed or in the diaper.

Head Banging

If he starts head banging, put him to bed on a mattress on the floor so there isn't a wall or headboard to bang against. Head banging gives some children a buzz, especially if it gets your attention. Try to ignore it. There is little or no chance of it causing any lasting problems in children with normal development.

Breath-Holding

Ignore him. Children usually only do this with an audience, so don't give him one. Children who hold their breath in temper usually change color, eventually faint and are unconscious for a short time. This always ends the breath-holding and your child is back to normal in a few seconds.

Vomiting

Your child literally may scream himself sick. Don't fuss over him when he's sick, even if it has ruined the carpet. Go in with two towels. Use one to wipe up the vomit and the other to put over the damp spot. Don't talk to your child or tell him what a bad boy he has been. And don't look your child in the face. Say your usual goodnight phrase and leave the room.

The Three-Day Sleep Plan—Step by Step

1. Tell your child what will happen. Explain that when you have said goodnight, no one will come into his bedroom until morning.
2. Talk it over with the rest of the people in your house: your partner, other children. Explain it won't be easy. If necessary, tell the neighbors why they might hear your child crying and screaming.
3. Make sure other important adults will back you up. The support of friends and relatives is vital. Try to find somebody who has succeeded by not responding to their child crying at night. It will reassure you that you are not the only one to try this method.
4. Choose a time when you don't need a lot of sleep yourself, such as a Friday or Saturday night when you or your partner aren't working the next day.
5. Arrange the room so you can see what your child is doing in the room—without him seeing you. Make sure his bed can be seen from the door. Put a peephole in the door so you can look in on him or hang a mirror on the wall so you can see him without him seeing you. Be able to check on your child without actually going into the room.
6. Put your child to bed using the normal bedtime routine.
7. Make sure your child has been to the bathroom and had a small evening drink. If you don't give him a drink, he might say he's thirsty, but if the drink is too big, he'll demand a trip to the bathroom. Cover yourself against such blackmail!
8. Say goodnight in the usual way and leave the room.
9. Don't give in to your child's attention-demanding tactics.

Eventually, your child will fall asleep. It might take 10 minutes or it might take an hour or longer. But if you persevere with your side of the bargain—not to go in—he *has* to give in first by falling asleep with exhaustion.

If you stick to this plan, it always works. I have never known it to take more than three nights to see a massive improvement.

Tip ✶ ✶ ✶ ✶ ✶ ✶ ✶ ✶ ✶ ✶ ✶ ✶ ✶ ✶ ✶ ✶ ✶ ✶ ✶

Oil the door hinges to his bedroom so if you do need to open the door to check on your child, they won't creak and give you away.

But: If you start this approach and then give up halfway through, you may be worse off than before you started. If you go in to your child after he has been crying for an hour, for example, he may continue crying for another hour tomorrow night because he knows you will come in eventually.

The Three-Day Sleep Plan is rapid and effective, but if you panic and stop swimming, you may drown.

Warning!

The Three-Day Sleep Plan, a rapid approach to creating a good sleep habit, has one particular risk: If you start in a determined way and then give up halfway through, you could find that the problems are worse rather than better. If you change your mind about diving into the cold water, you could do a belly flop! If you leave your child alone to cry for 30 minutes and then go in because you can't stand it anymore, your child will cry 30 minutes the next night because he knows he can win your attention.

If there is a danger you might give up halfway through the 3-day program, then arrange extra support to cover this high-risk time. Very few parents can manage the 3-day program entirely alone. Most people need a supportive spouse, friend, relative, healthcare practitioner or doctor.

Make sure you gather all the support you need before you start the Three-Day Sleep Plan (or any of the methods in the *Baby and Toddler Sleep Program*).

Common Questions and Issues

"I can't go through with this."

You may feel this way on the first night. But by the second, it becomes easier. And by the third, you'll be surprised at how easily he accepts that even if he yells, you're not going to cave into his demands. Remember:

- ☼ You have to set boundaries. Children actually like them—even if they don't follow them. If you allowed a child to do whatever he wanted, he'd feel lost eventually.

- ☼ Babies (over 6 months old) and toddlers are not harmed by crying (if the only reason for crying is that they want to be with you). Your child probably cries and screams during the day. That doesn't harm him. So what is different about nighttime?

- ☼ Research shows that before the age of 3, a child forgets what has happened to him. He won't have bad memories of being left to cry for a short time. (How much can *you* remember clearly before you were 3 or even 4 years old?)

- ☼ If your child is crying hard, he is healthy and has a lot of energy. The most appropriate time to worry about your child is when he *stops* crying and all is quiet. You may want to turn on the baby monitor and listen for quiet, regular, breathing sounds.

"It feels mean to be so tough."

Hardening your heart to the sound of your child crying goes against all your instincts. So remind yourself why it's important. You're teaching your child to sleep well. You are giving him advantages that will last a lifetime. He will

- ☼ Be secure with himself at night

- ☼ Learn to stay safe in one place when you tell him to

- ☼ Feel more secure and self-confident during the day

- ☼ Develop self-control

- ☼ Concentrate better

- ☼ Follow your directions

Why Stick with It?

✧ If you don't, you might end up with a compromised sleep habit. It might be bearable and just livable. But it won't be as effective as a good sleep routine.

✧ If you can't be firm with your child about bedtime, how will you cope in a truly dangerous situation at other times? If you do cope well with dangerous situations, use the same approach to get your child to sleep.

Billy

Billy's parents had read that most babies sleep through the night before they reach the age of 6 months. But Billy was now 6 months old and there was no sign he would sleep through the night. They decided to have him sleep in a crib by their bed so they could see he was all right. They found if Billy cried, he would calm down after a snuggle or a feeding. Breastfeeding was so successful, his mother used it to calm him, day or night. The problem was, Billy's mom had had 6 months of sleep deprivation and was depressed, irritable and rapidly running out of energy.

The doctor explained that Billy had been allowed to get into a routine that suited him, but didn't suit his parents. They realized it was better to do something sooner rather than later, so they gradually moved to a more regular feeding routine during the day. At night they moved him out of their bedroom and give him a stuffed animal for company. They were amazed when Billy started sleeping through the night. When he cried, he learned quickly to soothe himself back to sleep.

When Billy was just over 1 year old he had a nasty cough and cold, and he woke up frequently during the night. His parents went in several times during the night to comfort him. When he recovered, Billy continued to cry and scream on and off. He wouldn't stop until one or the other parent went into the room. He would stop as soon as they lifted him out of the crib and would start again as soon as they put him down again. This went on for 3 weeks and there was no sign of it getting any better.

Billy's parents tried to let him cry. But they were unable to because of his screams. Eventually, after much heart-searching they decided they would put Billy in the most soundproof room in the house—the kitchen. The parents made sure everything was safe and set up the baby monitor. They turned it on only when they wanted to check on Billy, and then they switched it off again.

It was hard for Billy's parents to get to sleep at first, but then they slept right through the night for the first time. They woke in a panic, worried about Billy. They rushed to the kitchen and found him smiling and waving his toy around. Billy had moved to another stage in his development toward independence.

Preparing for What Can Go Wrong

It is important to prepare the ground for Three-Day Sleep Plan by considering what could possibly go wrong. Hopefully the worst-case scenario never happens. But if it does, you need to be ready.

> We recommend minimum intervention.

Wetting the bed, head banging, breath-holding and vomiting—all while angry—may occur as a form of protest. The less attention you give to a protest, the less likely it is to occur again. We recommend minimum intervention. You may feel it is too harsh. If you do, you can manage these problems differently. But remember—the more attention you give, the more likely the problems will occur again.

The tough approaches recommended in *Baby and Toddler Sleep Program* can only be justified in the context of a loving family—where parents are confident their child is safe and healthy, and when they decide to help their child onto the next ladder rung toward independence.

Common Questions and Issues

"I'm worried that my child hurts his lungs when he cries."

This does not happen. In fact, his crying shows you his lungs are in perfect working order!

"What if he cries himself sick to get my attention?"

If your child is sick, clean up the mess quietly without saying anything. Change your child's clothes or bedding if necessary but don't talk. Then leave the room. The idea is to not to give him the attention he wants. Otherwise, he will be sick regularly.

"I don't like to see my child get upset."

This is totally understandable. But there is no evidence crying damages a child emotionally. Sooner or later, children are faced with a situation where they can't have what they want. It's better to tackle this moment in a safe, controlled environment. And it's best if *you* pick the time, such as bedtime.

There is also evidence that children exposed to carefully controlled stressful situations show greater competence and resilience. Children who are overprotected are challenged to earn their independence later in life.

Eventually, all parents have to teach their children that their demanding cries will not be automatically and immediately met. Every parent reaches the point when it is just not possible to respond to their child's cries. It is best to cross this bridge during the child's first few years of life.

Is Crying Harmful?

A crying baby is not the same as a crying grownup. Crying is the only means of expression for a tiny baby. Toddlers and even older children use crying to get what they want. But as children grow older they have to learn that crying has a powerful effect on people and is only to be used as a way of expressing emotions—sadness, misery, happiness or joy.

Babies and toddlers quickly learn to use their crying in a manipulative way. Crying has the power to control parents. Nature has designed us to react quickly to a child's cries of distress. This is how it should be. However, sometimes

Continued . . .

children use their crying to control and manipulate, and it is best to ignore this type of crying.

To ignore the crying of a child who has good cause to be distressed could be harmful. In fact, it is a form of emotional abuse. To ignore a crying child who is demanding attention and being manipulative is justifiable. Responding to this type of crying is harmful because it makes your child *more* likely to use crying to manipulate people.

Maria

Maria was a 2-year-old who had terrible temper tantrums 2 or 3 times a day, when she was asked to do something she didn't want to. There wasn't a pattern to the tantrums and most of the time she would follow the bedtime routine.

The tantrums were severe. Sometimes she would bang her head. Other times she would hit and kick anyone who happened to be near, and she would push over furniture and damage it. When Maria's parents discussed her behavior with their friends, they learned that tantrums are common at Maria's age. They felt better, but they still wondered how to cope with it.

> To ignore the crying of a child who has good cause to be distressed could be harmful. In fact, it is a form of emotional abuse.

The most frequent advice they received was to ignore the tantrums. They tried, but it only seemed to make the tantrums worse. Eventually, they discovered if they either turned their backs on her when she was having a tantrum, or walked out of the room (when they knew she was safe), the tantrum would end quickly. If they tried to move her somewhere else or pick her up, she usually got worse. The only other approach that worked was to hold her firmly until she exhausted herself. This usually made the tantrum go on much longer than it would have otherwise. She would eventually calm down and would be tranquil and self-controlled for several hours.

They finally decided to let Maria have her tantrum entirely on her own. Then they followed the bedtime routine. By the time Maria was tucked in bed, she was calm and soon off to sleep.

Tip
Rearrange your child's bedroom so it's a novelty for him to go to bed. New sheets or a cartoony pillowcase might make him want to climb into bed.

"I still can't cope. What should I do?"

If you can cope with your child crying for 3 minutes, let him cry that long. Then go in, show him you're there and go out again.

Every evening, increase the time by 1 or 2 minutes, according to how much you can take. Alternatively, you might feel strong enough to give the Three-Day Sleep Plan (pages 68 to 70) another try.

"I don't have enough energy to be firm and do what I know is best."

Get more help and support from friends, relatives or from parent-support groups. Perhaps your doctor or healthcare practitioner can help you.

"I feel guilty if I am tough on my child."

All parents feel guilty at one time or another, because parenting is impossible to get right all of the time. Don't worry too much. Do something nice with your child during the day to make up for the night before.

"I always start off with good intentions but then crack."

Work out in advance what makes you crack. Then plan ahead to avoid this problem next time. Are you tired and don't have the strength to continue? If so, go to bed earlier. If necessary, get help. Ask your partner to come home early or a friend to come over—it could take only 3 days to get this right, remember.

"I'm too fed up to be bothered with this anymore."

You probably have a good reason for feeling this way. Can you sort it out and deal with the cause of your misery? If not, it's wise to ask your family doctor for help.

"I'm too busy."

That's a shame for your child. Parenting takes time. And developing good sleep habits pays off in the end.

"I don't believe children should get upset."

That is a shame for you. There is no way of avoiding it so you are bound to be disappointed.

"I get my child to sleep by telling him I'm nearby. Then I do little jobs like ironing on the landing. Is this wrong?"

It's one way of dealing with it, but it won't solve the problem. You have to tackle the "crunch time" when you've finished the ironing and your child is still awake and doesn't want you to go away.

"I can only get my child to stay quietly in bed if I put him in the same bed or room as his brother."

That's not fair to the sibling: It may interfere with his own sleep pattern and independence. And it might encourage the two of them to play instead of resting.

"I don't have enough bedrooms for my child to have his own room. He has to share with his brother. How can I get them to sleep without playing?"

Be firm. Treat them as if they were in separate rooms. Tell them it's against the rules to talk. And if they start to get out of bed, do exactly what we've advised in previous chapters—take them back to bed with minimum talk or attention.

"I can only get my child to sleep if I play a recorded story tape. What's wrong with that?"

Eventually the tape ends. You may be lucky and find your child has drifted off. But if not, then what? Again, you're better off trying the rapid approach without a tape. If you must have one, fade out the tape every evening with shorter stories so your child eventually learns to go to sleep on his own.

Sharing Bedrooms

Lots of children share bedrooms. It's not always something you have a choice about if space is limited. So how can you put a sleep program into action if your nonsleeping child is sharing a bedroom with a child who wants to sleep? Or, even worse, how can you coax 2 nonsleepers to bed if one is jumping in and out of bed—and encouraging the other to do the same?

It's difficult, but by no means impossible. Do the following:

☽ Stick to your routine. Hang on to this word, "routine"! It's worth its weight in gold!

☽ Pretend each child is in a separate room. In other words, treat each one individually and act exactly the same as you would if he were in a room of his own.

☽ "Divide and rule." Put one child to bed in another place. Even if you don't have a spare bedroom, there's always the sofa, Grandma's house, or a friend's.

☽ Follow the Three-Day Sleep Plan outlined step-by-step earlier in the chapter to get the nonsleeping child to rest. It is only for 3 days. Then the other child could come back to his own bed.

Letting your child cry might sound tough, but it works. The softer, slower methods mentioned earlier might feel better in the short term, but you could be stuck with them long after your child goes to school.

Only you—and your partner—can decide what to do. But remember: Nothing ventured, nothing gained! If you don't try it, you won't know how well it works.

Tip · ★

☽ Keep a record to show what time you started the bedtime routine and what time your child eventually went to sleep. (See the Daily Checklist in chapter 1.)

5

Waking Up during the Night

Congratulations! You've done it. Your small, reluctant sleeper has gone to bed. You've followed your bedtime routine to the letter. You've stopped him from running downstairs and you've persevered through that difficult "let-him-cry" stage.

Your child's reward is he's finally fallen asleep. When he stays asleep through the night, he wakes up refreshed, alert and happy the next day. He doesn't feel grumpy and hyperactive because he's overtired and hasn't had enough rest. In other words, you have a nicer child.

Your reward for all your effort is, you finally have an evening to yourself. Remember what the word "evening" used to mean in the days before children—a chance to unwind at the end of the day, an opportunity to talk to your partner about things that have nothing to do with children, time to enjoy a meal, read a book or simply collapse in front of the television.

So far, so good . . . until your child decides to wake up during the night. Don't panic! All is not lost. It *doesn't* mean your child has won the sleep battle after all. It means you have to follow a set routine to get him back into bed just as you did to get him into bed in the first place.

When your child wakes up during the night, the chances are you'll be asleep. That's a problem. People vary in how fast they become alert when someone wakes them up. Some of us take a half-hour plus a cup of coffee to really feel awake. Others jump up immediately and then feel awful later. But most people resent being awakened from a sound sleep.

This leaves parents in a dangerously vulnerable frame of mind. You're tired. You don't want to spend a half-hour coaxing your baby or toddler back to sleep. Why isn't your child asleep? Everyone else's child is . . .

Stop! Despite what friends might tell you about their children sleeping through the night, it's not true for every child. Patterns change, too. A baby often learns to sleep for 4 or 5 hours at a time before he's 6 months old and then suddenly, at age 2, he starts to wake up for no apparent reason.

Tip . . . .

A good way to reassure yourself that you are not the only one awake at night is to picture yourself looking down from the sky at a town. Look at all the lights on in the middle of the night. Peer through the windows and see all the other parents trying to soothe a baby or child back to sleep.

The truth is, a lot of children wake up during the night. Otherwise, there wouldn't be a demand for a book like this. But if parents had more help knowing what to do when their children woke, they'd be able to get them back to bed again. And this is exactly what we're going to do now.

Is It Normal to Wake Up during the Night?

The answer is "yes." Adults do it, too. We all sleep in cycles, starting with a shallow cycle, then a deep cycle and then a shallow one again, and so on. The amount of time spent in each cycle depends on one's age. Preschool children usually go from shallow to deep and then to shallow within an hour. School-age children take about 1½ hours. Adults usually sleep in 2- to 3-hour cycles.

A child naturally goes through what is called *rapid eye movement (REM) sleep*. REM is also called *active sleep* because it is the time when dreams occur. Information from daytime experiences is sorted and stored in long-term memory during REM. Babies spend about 50% of their sleeping time in REM sleep. They may make sucking movements, twitch and smile. If his eyes flicker open, you might mistakenly think your child is awake. If your child appears to be looking at you during the REM cycle, you might be tempted to talk to him, ask if he's all right or wake him up.

Your child may stir and move around when he returns to the shallow cycle. He may even cry. Learn to curb the natural tendency to rush in to see what's wrong.

Why? Because *you also* wake up in the night when you reach your shallow cycle, but over the years, you've learned to turn over and go back to sleep. Supposing, however, someone came in and patted you on the shoulder, asked if you were all right and offered you a drink. Wouldn't that wake you up? Probably. Most likely you'd feel more reluctant to go back to sleep—especially if you hadn't really wanted to go to bed in the first place.

It's the same for your child. Providing your child is both healthy and safe, he's more likely to go back to sleep on his own if you let him stir a little and even cry without going in and checking on him.

What to Do if My Child Wakes Up

You have two options. You can let him cry, or you can see what is wrong. The first option might sound tough. As usual, only let him cry if he is both healthy and safe. By 6 months, most children have a definite pattern of waking during the day and sleeping during the night, so it is a reasonable time to start letting your child cry. Here are the advantages of allowing a child over the age of 6 months to cry at night:

☆ Your child is likely to go back to sleep when his body naturally takes him into the next stage (the deep cycle). He learns that although he may wake up, it's surprisingly easy to go back to sleep on his own. If you go in, give him a drink, talk to him or get him up, you interrupt his natural sleep cycle.

☆ Your child develops the habit of waking up when you check on him and he becomes aware you are in the room.

☆ Most children discover they can control you by crying. There is nothing wrong with this because crying continues to be an important way to signal for help, but children have to learn to use this for communicating a problem, *not* for manipulating people. You teach your child an important lesson by not responding to these crying demands for attention during the night.

✧ You give your child a clear message that you are in control when you don't respond to his unreasonable demands for your undivided attention during the night. Unfortunately, children who always have their demands met soon take control themselves and become unlikable—and it's only because their parents allowed it to happen.

✧ Children who feel their parents are in control of them, rather than the other way around, feel more secure.

Caroline

Caroline was 18 months old and frequently cried during the night. Her parents had been told to let her to cry in her room and had tried this on several occasions. They could only listen to the crying for about 5 minutes before they decided it was too cruel to allow her to continue. Their parents told them that children who were left to cry became emotionally disturbed later. The longest wait they ever managed was 20 minutes, and they felt really upset afterward. Caroline also was distressed and cried even more.

The parents were confused by the conflicting advice they had received. They consulted a child psychiatrist. She told them that by allowing Caroline to cry for 20 minutes occasionally and then for shorter periods other times, they actually encouraged her to cry, because Caroline knew her parents would eventually come in. The psychiatrist told them there was no evidence that letting a child cry alone would cause emotional damage, provided the child was safe, healthy and there were no obvious causes for the crying.

She shared research that showed children benefited from coping with stressful events that were carefully managed and supervised by their parents. In spite of this reassurance, Caroline's parents still felt uncomfortable about leaving her alone to cry. They decided to take the slow approach and allow Caroline to cry for a minute longer on each occasion before going in to her. This worked well at first. However, they seemed to be making very little progress. Caroline seemed to be getting worse rather than better. It became so difficult they decided to stop for a few weeks and then start again.

Next time around was easier, but it wasn't long before Caroline was crying again for long periods. At this point her father decided to take control and let Caroline cry as long as she wanted. Caroline's mother found this extremely difficult to cope with. The first night was so distressing she decided to use earplugs. When she awoke the next morning, she was surprised to hear Caroline had slept right through the night and was delighted when this continued.

Still Worried?

You can always listen in on the monitor or hover outside to make sure your child is all right. But don't let him realize you're there or you blow your cover!

Parenthood isn't easy. It's hard to wrap that present for your child's future when the paper doesn't fold neatly. But when you persevere, you make the present look wonderful. When you give yourself and your child good sleep habits, you both enjoy each other's company more during the day because you are well-rested.

Being Your Child's Only Comfort

Your toddler is crying. Does he want a drink? Does he want a hug? What could be more natural? Again, that's fine *if that's what you want*. But remember—when you go in, tuck him in and give him a drink, he is more likely to wake up during the shallow sleep cycle. Then he needs your presence to get back to sleep.

In other words, you become his only comfort. You might not mind that at the moment. You may even find it comforting to know your child is awake and needs you. Parenthood is scary business, especially when it's dark and fears get out of proportion. You look after your children all day and then at night, you expect them to handle themselves. But the truth is, they can.

Did you know?

Research shows the more a parent tries to make a child go to sleep, the less likely it is the child will sleep through the night.

The less interference, the better!

Common Questions and Issues

"I can't stand hearing him cry at night."

You're conditioned to respond when a child cries. But remember—to wake up is normal, and to fall back to sleep is natural. When both sleeping children and adults are filmed, they wake up, move around and open their eyes during the shallow cycle and then go back to sleep again.

Picture your child having a meal. He's sitting at a table eating a plate of nutritious food, which you've lovingly prepared for him. You wouldn't snatch it away from him, would you? Similarly, don't take his sleep away from him by disturbing him when he's sleeping lightly. You'll be taking away all the goodness that sleep and rest can bring.

Even if your child cries during the shallow phase, it doesn't necessarily mean he's upset. Babies and even toddlers often find crying comforting. It's familiar. It's almost like talking to themselves. You probably make little noises yourself during the night.

By now, you are able to recognize the kind of cry your child is making from its sound. You know from experience whether it's a "Help—something-awful-is-happening" cry or a tired cry that quickly peters out. If your child has worked himself up and is really yelling, but you know he is healthy and safe, comfort yourself by realizing that if he's crying that loudly, there can't be anything wrong with his lungs or energy level. Perhaps he's going to be a good singer one day . . .

All children soothe themselves sooner or later. But always make sure they are safe and feeling OK before you leave them alone to cry.

Did you know?

Babies can be divided into self-soothers and nonself-soothers. Those who soothe themselves wake and go quietly to sleep again. Self-soothers are more likely to use a stuffed animal, a blanket or a thumb. Nonself-soothers wake and cry out. They are more likely to depend on their parents to quiet them.

"How old should my baby be before I let him cry himself back to sleep?"

As a rough guide, always go in to a crying baby under 6 months. But between 6 months and a year, he sleeps longer between the hours of midnight and 5 A.M. than he used to. A clear pattern of daytime waking and nighttime sleeping is also formed. This is when to start helping him help himself go back to sleep.

Also, by this time, you know your child and are able to work out the difference between a genuine cry for help and an attention-seeking cry. Obviously this isn't going to happen overnight, so play it by ear. But the sooner you start, the more effective it is.

"What if my child is hungry?"

From 6 months onwards, your child's body is automatically prepared to cope without food for 5 or 6 hours during the night. If you offer a bottle or a drink, he'll assume you will do this every time he wakes up. He'll get into the habit of wanting a nightcap! If you continue to feed him during the night, he may also put on too much weight.

"What if my child is thirsty?"

If you ignore a toddler's cries for a drink, you're not being cruel. He won't die of thirst or hunger by not having a drink for a few hours. Think of it this way: Occasionally you wake in the night feeling hungry, especially if you didn't eat dinner the night before. But it doesn't hurt you if you turn over and go back to sleep. All that happens is you are more likely to want breakfast in the morning.

Alternatively, you could leave a small plastic container of water next to his bed so he can help himself. But make sure it's water. Anything tastier—such as milk or fruit juice—will make him realize it's worth his while to wake up. Fruit juice "on tap" through the night is also bad for his teeth.

"I can't leave him alone to cry but my partner says I should."

Ask your partner to take over responsibility for your crying child and for comforting you when your child cries. Maybe your partner doesn't realize how much it is affecting you, especially if you tend to be the waking partner.

It's a sad fact that some marriages run into difficulty after the birth of a child because couples disagree on how to bring up their child. (See also chapter 11.) A crying child produces very strong emotions in parents. It is easy for arguments to develop when you are in an emotional state.

Apart from talking it out, there aren't any easy solutions. Discuss sleep just as you would discuss other areas like eating, learning to walk and learning to talk. Listen to each other's views. You might learn something yourself if you're open to another point of view. Try to reach a compromise.

If you can't, why not try it his or her way? If that doesn't work, try the other method. Don't let your child's sleep problems creep into your bedroom life.

Read this book together and support each other in following the guidelines. If you follow them carefully, they work.

Tip

You can tell which parent is the "soft," indulgent one because your child will always go to that side of the bed, even if it means walking around the bed.

"It's easier to let him into our bed."

You're tired. It's the middle of the night. You need your sleep too. It's so much easier to let him into your bed, but there are drawbacks:

- ❄ It won't help him become independent and develop good sleep habits in the long run.

- ❄ It can prevent you from sleeping. If your child is still a baby, you may not sleep well because you are afraid you might roll over and hurt him. If he's a toddler, he may wiggle. By morning, you may wake up feeling as though you haven't had any sleep.

Think of it this way. If you're short on cash, you could take control of your finances or you could borrow money. Borrowing would make you feel better for a short time, but the more you borrow, the more interest you have to pay back. The longer it goes on, the worse it gets.

It's the same with sleep habits. The more you look for quick and easy solutions by "borrowing" peace and quiet, the harder it is going to be in the long run.

"It feels mean to leave him in his bed crying."

Try this slower, alternative approach: Stand at your child's door without saying anything, or sit quietly by his bed, out of reach. He can see you there. He knows you're around. But he also knows you're not going to start the day in the middle of the night. After a few minutes, go back to your own bed. On each occasion, reduce the amount of time you stay.

The trouble with this method is that even a small glimpse of you may make him worse. If he yells again, you might come back. Remember—quick and easy solutions often have a high cost in the long run.

"My partner has to work in the morning. If we let our child cry, we'll be too tired to cope."

Rethink everyone's sleeping places. For example, the working partner can sleep in the spare bedroom or sofa for a few nights. It won't be for long—just until your child learns he can go back to sleep on his own. Alternatively, move your child so his cries aren't so loud in your bedroom. But remember, wherever your child is, he must be safe.

"I can't stand the noise."

Buy a pair of earplugs. Your child will stop screaming sooner than you think. It's amazing how 60 seconds of yelling can seem more like 60 minutes when it's at full volume!

Tip

If you find it hard to take your child back to bed, try swapping sides. Your child is used to coming to your side of the bed for sympathy. If he comes to the wrong side, your partner can take him back.

If your partner doesn't want to be disturbed because he or she is going to work the next day, save this method for weekends.

Wandering Out of Bed

Waking up in the night is one thing. But getting out of bed is an entirely different ball game. Go back to the rulebook. You and your partner must agree on the rules. During the day, you're probably watching your toddler most of the time. We all know they're capable of doing some pretty terrible things within seconds.

If your toddler or older child wakes up at night and starts wandering around the house when you are asleep, it could be very dangerous for him. If you are worried about your child's safety, make sure

✷ There's a gate on your child's bedroom door—and he's not able to climb over it.

✷ The house is safe. Has anyone left pill bottles, razors or medicines within reach?

✷ Your child can't interfere with electric or gas controls.

✷ There are no fires or anything hot, such as electrical heaters, that could harm him.

✷ He can't get through any windows or doors.

Build Your Own Home Alarm Kit!

It's important—for safety reasons—to know when your toddler is wandering around at night, especially if you are a deep sleeper and unlikely to hear him come out of his room. Here are some tips that help:

✷ Put an alarm system on his door, so you'll know if he comes out. Buy one from a hardware store or make your own by hanging a little bell on the knob or door so the door disturbs it if opened.

✷ Tie a bunch of saucepans to the child's bedroom door and put them on a chair. When the door opens, the pans will fall onto the floor with a crash!

✷ Keep your baby monitor on—resist the temptation to rush in if you hear the usual shallow-cycle waking noises.

Jason

Jason was a very determined 4-year-old. His parents found it particularly difficult to divert him from anything he decided to do. Unfortunately, Jason decided he didn't want to sleep in his bedroom. He preferred to sleep in his parents' bedroom—preferably in their bed, between them. Jason's parents knew the they had to be firm and set clear limits. In Jason's case, this only made matters worse.

What started off as a simple disagreement got out of hand, and Jason sulked and tried to do what he wanted anyway. Whatever the parents tried, Jason always seemed to end up in their bed. His father was fed up and determined not to be beaten by a 4-year-old. He decided he would stay quietly outside Jason's bedroom door and return him to bed every time he tried to come out. Jason behaved like a "jack-in-the-box" for the rest of the evening and was still coming out at midnight, although it wasn't as frequent as earlier in the evening. At this point Jason's father decided to sleep outside Jason's bedroom to make sure Jason knew his parents were in control and not him. Jason's father slept outside the bedroom door for a week, although Jason got the message after 4 nights.

Common Questions and Issues

"What do I do if my child starts wandering around the house?"

Remember when you put him to bed and he kept coming down to see what you were up to? You didn't talk to him. You walked him in front of you back to his room. Your expression was serious. And you used key words like "Back to bed." (See page 47.)

Now do exactly the same, even if your brain is only half working because you're half asleep. Escort him back to bed and say your magic goodnight phrase firmly but kindly: "Good night, sleep tight." If he gets out of bed, do the same thing again and again. Don't allow this to be repeated too many times.

Tip

Keep a flashlight by your bedside. If you hear your child wandering around in the night, you have a light to guide him back to bed. This is better than turning on the bedroom light, which wakes him up even more.

"But he needs the bathroom."

If your toddler isn't potty-trained and he's damp, use an extra diaper the next night. Change your diaper brand or put an extra liner in. Research shows toddlers don't usually wake because they are wet. In fact, they usually wet just as they are waking up.

Keep a spare set of clean pajamas handy so you don't wake him up even more by turning on the lights to look for clean clothes. Change him if necessary without speaking. This is no time for chatting. The reason for this is, the more he wakes up, the more likely it will become part of his sleep pattern.

If your child is toilet-trained and wants to use the bathroom, that's fair enough—but only once. If he needs it continually, it's probably an excuse. To make sure, take him to the doctor. Perhaps he has a urinary problem. (See also pages 102-103.)

"He has a stomachache."

Is it an excuse or does he mean it? If he's really sick, you'll know soon enough. If it's a stomachache every night, he's either fooling you or he needs to see the doctor.

"He's afraid of the dark."

If he's always been used to dark rooms, this won't happen. But, if not, use a dim bulb or a dimmer switch to gradually fade out the light as the days and weeks go by. Traditionally we're taught to be afraid of the dark. But you can teach children that the dark is comforting. The more you feed the fear—by leaving the light on—the worse it gets. Keeping the light on gives your child the message that the dark is dangerous.

"There's a monster in his room!"

Of course there isn't! Look under the bed. See, there's nothing there! If you look under the bed or draw back the curtains to show nothing is hiding, you perpetuate the myth that something may be there in the first place. Instead, simply say, "Things like that don't exist" or words to that effect.

Be careful what movies and television your child watches. It is proved that what children watch can have a bad effect on them and can make some children very anxious. Fears of monsters and darkness are most frequent between the ages of 4 and 6 and affect as many as 80% of children.

"We only have one bedroom so our child has to share our room."

Follow the rules as if he were in his own room. If your child cries, don't get up. Wait it out. Take him back to bed if he gets out. Or create a partition by hanging a curtain across the room so his bed or crib is on one side and your bed is on the other. If he doesn't see you, he might to go back to sleep more easily.

"My child gets into my bed but I don't notice until I wake up."

This sounds more like your problem than his! Be careful—if he can get in undetected, so might anyone. Perhaps it's time to buy a burglar alarm. Also remember that adult beds can be dangerous for children. They aren't designed with children in mind. It is possible for your child to fall out or get smothered.

"He climbs into the other children's beds."

This might sound like a good idea—especially if it lets you sleep. But it's not fair to his siblings. They need a good night's rest too. They won't rest if a small, fidgety toddler wakes them up.

"I can't stop checking on my child at night."

The irony is that when your little one does eventually begin to sleep for a decent stretch of time, your body is aware of his nocturnal movements. Even though he may be sleeping soundly, you may wake up and wonder if he's all right.

If you check on him, you could wake him, especially if he's going through the shallow stage of the sleep cycle. Then you're back where you started.

Try to be rational. If your child weren't all right, he'd be yelling. It's natural to check on small babies regularly, but as your child grows up, become more confident about knowing when he is strong enough to manage without you. Most parents know their toddlers well enough to let them sleep through the night without checking.

Tip

Talk to your child in whispers. It reinforces the idea that night is for resting, sleeping and not playing. And it calms you down so you're not tempted to say loudly, "Why are you out of bed?" If you are calm, he's more likely to be calm too—and more willing to go back to bed.

6

Nighttime Problems

Night is a funny time. Some people find the darkness soothing; others find it exaggerates fears they have during the
day. How will I tackle that business meeting tomorrow?
How will I get everything done at home?

Nighttime has a similar effect on our attitude toward parenting. Being a mother or father can be a lot of fun. But it's also
scary. We have a responsibility to bring up our children safely. No
one has really shown us how to do it. It's like starting a new job
without direction.

The dark makes fears even worse, especially if you haven't
learned to relax when your child is asleep in one room and you're
in another. All sorts of worries flash through your mind: "Is my
daughter ill? She was warm when I put her to bed." Or, "What
was that noise? Could my son be choking?"

Here's a list of some common nighttime behavior patterns
you should be aware of, with practical advice on how to handle
them. Many of them are perfectly normal.

Nightmares

These usually occur in the second two-thirds of the night, normally just before waking. They happen most commonly as part of

a developmental phase between the age of 2 and the teenage years. About half of all 5-year-olds have nightmares, although they decrease with age, and are usually a passing phase.

Nightmares occur more often if a child is anxious or stressed. A traumatic event, a frightening television program or movie or some medicines can also cause them. Most nightmares have no obvious cause and no special significance. However, if the same nightmare recurs night after night, it may have meaning for the child.

What to do

✡ Go in and reassure your child with the "magic" bedtime phrase. Reassure him everything is all right. Tuck him in gently and leave the room as soon as you can.

✡ Keep a chart. Is your child having nightmares for a particular reason? Is he worried about school or another child? Is there a pattern to the nightmares?

✡ Repeated nightmares can often be controlled. For example, if the dream involves a monster chasing your child, work out a plan with your little one to deal with the monster. You could do this while he's still in bed. For example, you could suggest to your child that you could both make this monster fall into a hole, drown or get trapped in a cage. (This plan works because nightmares occur in the lighter stages of sleep, which makes dreams more easy to control. A child's imagination is also more adaptable than an adult's and open to suggestion.)

✡ In the morning, ask older children if they want to tell you about the nightmare. Talking about nightmares can sometimes help. If you dwell on them too much, however, it might increase the likelihood of repetition.

Rachel

Rachel was 6 years old when she was in a car accident. The car she was in was hit from behind by another car. Rachel's father, who was driving, had to be taken to the hospital for severe bruising. Rachel was examined in the emergency room before she was allowed to go home. For the next 6 weeks she didn't sleep well and most nights she would wake up screaming after a nightmare.

The nightmare was almost exactly the same each time and was about the accident. She was less active during the day than usual and her appetite was poor. She became much more tense and anxious and repeatedly talked about the accident and how it happened. Rachel's parents consulted their doctor, who explained that Rachel had typical symptoms of post-traumatic stress disorder.

The symptoms normally fade after 4 to 6 weeks. Fortunately, this happened for Rachel. She continued to have an occasional nightmare about the accident and was anxious when riding in a car, but she gradually improved over the next year.

> About half of all 5-year-olds have nightmares. Nightmares decrease as the child grows and are usually a passing phase.

Night Terrors

These are different from nightmares. They occur in the deepest part of sleep (during the first third of the night). Your child is agitated and moves around in his crib or bed. He appears to be awake but isn't. He seems very frightened, with rapid breathing and a fast heart rate. His eyes stare at you. It can be scary. What is wrong with your child?

The answer is: nothing. The experience is probably more frightening for you than for him because he doesn't know what he is doing. Research shows that children never remember night terrors in the morning.

What to do

☆ Don't wake him up. It's almost impossible to do and will upset both of you.

☆ Wait next to him patiently. The terror will soon pass. It usually only lasts a few minutes, but it could last up to 30 minutes.

☆ Tuck him in quietly and say the familiar bedtime phrase to reassure him.

✧ Keep a chart. If the terrors happen regularly, wake him up just before they're about to start so you interrupt the sleep cycle. Then coax him back to sleep again. If it continues, see your doctor.

✧ We've already said that your child won't remember his night terror in the morning. So don't worry too much.

Ben

Ben was 5 years old when he started waking up around 11 P.M. His parents would be startled by a blood-curdling yell. They would rush in to see what had happened to Ben. He would be sitting up in bed looking scared to death, with wide-open, staring eyes, waving his arms to fight off an imaginary monster. Ben's parents tried to calm him but whatever they did seemed to make things worse or have no effect at all.

After consulting their doctor, who told them Ben was having night terrors, his parents learned to stay calm with Ben during the night terror and to keep him from hurting himself. When the terror passed, they could simply tuck him in bed and leave the room. When asked, Ben was completely unaware of what had happened during the night. Fortunately the phase passed in a few months and Ben only had 10 night terrors in all. His schoolwork and his general development were unaffected.

Did you know?

Night terrors are more common in boys. They also run in families.

Sleepwalking

Like night terrors, sleepwalking occurs in the first third of the night when your child is in a deep sleep. It also tends to run in families.

What to do

⚡ Do not wake your child. Lead him back to bed and make sure he settles. Tuck him in and say the "magic words."

⚡ Check to be sure there aren't any obstacles for him to fall over. Your child's safety is the most important thing. This is usually only a passing phase, so you'll be able to move things back the way they were in a little while.

⚡ If it happens regularly, make a chart and see if there's a particular pattern behind the sleepwalking.

Did you know?

Studies show 1 in 6 children sleepwalk at some stage—usually as they approach adolescence.

Snoring

Around 10% of children snore regularly. It may be a symptom of obstructive sleep apnea. Although this is a rare condition, it is important to recognize, because it causes problems for the child during the daytime.

Common symptoms of obstructive sleep apnea include

⚡ Snoring

⚡ Breath holding while asleep

⚡ Restlessness

⚡ Mouth breathing

⚡ Sleepiness during the day

⚡ Difficult, irritable behavior

⚡ Hyperactivity

It might be caused by

⚡ Airway obstruction; for example, tonsils and adenoids

⚡ Obesity

⚡ Blocked nose

⚡ Parental smoking

What to do

⭐ See your doctor.

Did you know?

Approximately 12% of children snore between the ages of 4 and 7. Children who snore are more likely to sleep during the day, be hyperactive and be restless sleepers. Snoring also usually decreases with age. So if your child is snoring at 5 years old, he'll probably stop by 7. If you're worried, see your doctor.

Sleep Talking

Sleep talking usually occurs in deep sleep and is not remembered.

What to do

Nothing! Sleep talking is perfectly natural. You might even learn a thing or two about your child's private life! However, most sleep talking is just mumbo-jumbo. Don't try to wake your child. If he is agitated, smooth his brow, say the "magic" bedtime phrase and help him to turn over and go back to sleep.

Nighttime Coughing and Sniffles

This is miserable for you and your child. You've managed to get him to sleep but you can't sleep well yourself because the cough is making him restless.

What to do

Check to be sure his room isn't too damp, dry, cold or hot. If he's coughing more when he's lying down, it could be due to large tonsils or what is known as a *post-nasal drip*. This occurs when the sinuses drain and the secretions trickle down the back of the throat. If the throat is irritated or there are large tonsils, the child may cough—especially when he is lying down.

Simple remedies include:

⭐ Help him sit up.

⭐ Give him a small sip of water or a honey drink to soothe the throat.

- Use a humidifier for younger children.
- Fill a basin with steaming water and help him hold his head over it (never touching) with a towel draped over his head so he inhales steam. Make sure the steam is not too hot for him. Even steam can burn!
- Raise the top end of the bed by placing bricks or books underneath. Jiggle it to make sure it is stable.
- If your child is old enough to have a pillow, give him an extra one so he sleeps with his chest raised, which allows him to breath better.
- Be wary of cough medicines. Most contain drugs that make children restless and irritable. There is no real evidence that any cough medicine is better than honey, water or any other simple remedy.

Coughing is not serious if your child:

- Feels physically OK
- Eats well
- Continues normal activity
- Breathes normally

Teeth Grinding

This is more common in older children and is worse in times of stress. It sounds unpleasant, but it doesn't have any special significance.

What to do

- Change the pillows—it may be enough to stop this particular bedtime habit. If necessary, alter the position of the bed. These changes can produce improved sleep habits.
- Visit the dentist. Continual teeth grinding can cause dental problems.

Bed Wetting

This isn't usually considered a problem until the child is 5 years old. Don't feel you're the only one who has a child with this problem. Almost 10% of all 5-year-olds wet their beds at night. It's more common in boys, and it runs in families.

Bed wetting is caused by

❧ Developmental delay or immaturity

❧ Bladder infections (rarely)

❧ Lack of training or delayed training

It's made worse by

❧ Stress of any kind, including excitement

What to do

❧ Make a reward chart with stickers for dry nights (For more ideas, see the section on Rewards in chapter 7).

❧ See your doctor, who might prescribe drugs that can help your child if he has to sleep away from home. However, all medicines only stop the symptoms and do not help bladder control to mature.

❧ Your doctor might prescribe an *enuretic alarm*. This is a battery-operated gadget that buzzes when the child is wet. It works on the principle that urine conducts electricity. There are two main alarm types. In one, a low-voltage electric current is conducted between two metal-and-gauze pads placed under the bed sheets. In the other type of alarm, current passes between contacts on a small electrode hidden in a pad in your child's pants.

The theory is the noise wakes your child when he starts to urinate, and he can then be trained to get up to go to the bathroom. Eventually, he will learn to do so without the buzz. The method has been found to be successful in 80% of cases.

☼ Reduce the amount of fluid your toddler drinks before going to bed. Explain why you are doing this. It probably won't stop the wetting but it will reduce the amount of urine passed.

☼ Avoid drinks like cola or tea containing caffeine, which stimulate urine production.

☼ Don't lift your toddler out of bed to take him to the bathroom before *you* go to sleep. This could interfere with his sleep cycle and wake him up! Nor does it train your child. He may leave responsibility for his bladder control to you.

☼ Follow the Dry Bed Method used in conjunction with an alarm (see box, below). This has been shown to have a 90% success rate in 6 weeks. But it's not easy!

The Dry Bed Method

Before bedtime help your child practice getting out of bed and going to the bathroom 20 times, counting up to 20 in bed and to 20 in the bathroom. On the first night wake up your child every hour, give him a drink and ask if he wants to go to the bathroom. If he does, praise him. But if he has an accident and wets the bed, he has to repeat the "20 times routine" and help change the sheets.

On following nights, encourage your child to drink normally. But when the buzzer sounds or he wakes up in a wet bed, he should go to the bathroom and then help change the sheets. If your child has wet the bed the night before, he has to repeat the "20 times routine" before going to bed at night.

Keep a record, and if your child is dry for 7 nights, remove the buzzer. But if he wets himself for two consecutive nights, return the buzzer. This intensive training method works by a technique called *overlearning*.

Colic

It's easy to mistake ordinary crying for colic. If you interfere too much, it encourages your child to wake up again and again. In fact, colic is normal between the ages of 3 to 4 months and only becomes a problem in about 15% of children. No real explanation has ever been found for its occurrence. It's possible that crying itself may cause air to be trapped in the stomach, causing pain.

What to do

☼ Simple remedies are best, such as giving your child a security blanket or a stuffed animal. Colic will pass.

☼ Check for any other cause for pain, such as diaper rash, thrush or earache. If in doubt, see your doctor.

Claire

Claire was 3 months old when her parents became concerned she had colic because her crying was so extreme. Their doctor told them excessive crying is common during the first 3 to 6 months. He told them it is considered colic if it occurs more than 3 days a week and totals more than 3 hours a day, and if the infant seems to be in pain and does not respond to soothing. The doctor said no one is really sure what causes colic, but it tends to improve with time. It is thought that a small minority of babies with colic have an allergic reaction to cow's milk. Feeding the baby differently can decrease the crying.

Persistent crying in the first 6 months is normal because babies are learning how to affect the world around them. Claire's parents were reassured by this explanation. They found it easier to cope with her crying because they knew the crying would improve on its own in 2 or 3 months.

Thumb-Sucking

About 20% of children under 5 years old suck their thumbs. Research also shows that thumb-suckers are more likely to use a blanket or a stuffed animal later on. There are pros and cons to thumb-sucking. On the plus side, a child who sucks his thumb is less likely to wake up at night—after all, he has his thumb to look after him!

On the minus side, the longer thumb-sucking continues, the more difficult it will be to "kick" the habit. Some children continue to suck their thumbs until they're 10, 11, 12 or even into their teens.

Thumb-sucking after the age of 3 or 4 may alter the way the mouth, jaws and teeth grow. And thumb-sucking during the day may interfere with communication. The child may be teased by other children.

What to do

✵ Keep your child's thumbs busy, away from his mouth. A mouth guard or an activity that keeps the hands occupied can be helpful.

Sleep Positions

Some children end up in the strangest positions when they're asleep! If you're worried, you could try to straighten him without waking him, but it might be your child's way of saying he's comfortable. You probably have your own peculiar sleep position.

What to do

✵ If your child tends to throw off the sheets or blankets and wakes up cold and shivering, invest in an all-in-one sleeper. If necessary, dress him in an extra sweater or sweatshirt. Layers can be useful in winter (vest, T-shirt, sweatshirt). But don't overheat a baby or young toddler.

Sudden Infant Death Syndrome (SIDS)

Many parents are tempted to check their babies and toddlers at night because they're afraid of SIDS. It's a fear many parents share, so don't think you're overreacting.

You can, however, stop worrying so much if you know you've done everything possible to prevent it.

What to do

✦ Breastfeed your baby. Studies show this reduces the risk of SIDS.

✦ Put your baby to sleep on his back. The latest research shows this is the best position. Lying on his chest may interfere with his breathing.

✦ Make sure your baby or younger toddler isn't too hot. Feel his skin. Is he wearing too much? Is the room very warm? As a guideline, he should feel a comfortable temperature without being either too hot or cold.

✦ Don't smoke—the same goes for your partner.

✦ Keep your baby in the room with you for the first 3 to 6 months. Although there is no evidence that this makes SIDS less likely, it helps you know what is happening with your child and whether he is ill or not.

Still worried? Remember some things are outside your control, such as:

✦ Infection

✦ Your child's immunity system not working efficiently

✦ Prematurity

If you are concerned about any of the above, consult your doctor. If there is a history of SIDS in your family, consult your doctor.

Try not to worry too much. Parenthood can be a scary business, but it can also be enjoyable. Concentrate on the fun you have with your child. Don't dwell on things that might go wrong.

7

Good Morning!

ou might wonder why we need a chapter on morning. After all, this is a book is about how to help your child *sleep*. By morning, it's too late. The fact is, morning is a good time to reflect on how you got your child to bed the night before and where you went wrong—or right.

Sometimes it helps to make a list. Use the Sleep Questionnaire on pages 14 to 16 to help you. What helped get your child to sleep eventually? What didn't help? Can you do the same things again?

It Isn't Morning Yet!

Parents often complain that they can get their children to sleep for most of the night, but their children wake up too early, at 5 or 6 A.M. One mother constantly complained that she was exhausted by having to start her day at the crack of dawn.

What to do

✵ Set a definite time to get up.

✵ Pretend it's 1 or 2 A.M.—even if it's later. Do exactly what you would do in the middle of the night. If your child is wandering around the house or hovering by your bed, take him back to bed. Use simple words and a firm voice. If your child is still in his crib, do what you would do in the middle of the night. Leave him alone to settle down. Let him learn to rest by himself.

⊰ You could go in and show your face to reassure him. If you do go in, however, your child is likely to continue to yell for you because he wants to see you again.

Tip ★ ★ ★ ★ ★ ★ ★ ★ ★ ★ ★ ★ ★ ★ ★ ★ ★ ★

☾ Buy your child his own alarm clock or lend him one. He's only allowed to get out of bed when the alarm goes off. Even toddlers can understand this. Make it a special present. Say, "Aren't you grown-up! You have your own alarm clock now."

Time to Get Up!

Children are wonders at moving the goal posts. Last night, they wouldn't go to bed. Now they don't want to get up in the morning!

If your children are at home all day, it might not matter too much. But sooner or later, they need to be at school by a certain time. And then you need to get yourself into a routine. Why not start now?

Of school-age children, almost a third need to be awakened for school in the morning. And if they need to be awakened, they might not be very alert for class because they are not getting enough sleep.

What to do

⊰ Organize a definite wake-up routine for the morning and stick to it, just as you do with the bedtime routine.

⊰ Bring the bedtime routine forward by an hour or a half-hour. If you child goes to bed earlier, he might get to sleep earlier and wake up when you want him to.

⊰ Give your child time to wake up. Children are like adults. Some are natural early birds. Others take time to get used to the waking world. If you let your child sleep in until the last possible moment you'll be in a rush to get to daycare, school or anything else you may have planned. Rushing invariably means a bad-tempered child, not to mention a bad-tempered adult. Is it worth it?

Tip

Wake up your child gently—at least 15 minutes before you really need him to get up. Turn on a radio or sing as you get his clothes out. It gives him time to "come to."

Rewards

Morning is also the time when you can praise your child for being so good during the night. When your child has done what you've asked, you can reward him for it. It's incentive to do it again. If someone gave you a bottle of wine or a raise in pay every time you cleaned the house well or wrote a good report, you'd try to do it again, wouldn't you? Even if your child has not stayed in bed and been quiet all night, it is important to find something you can praise and reward, such as "Good job, you got up one less time than the night before last."

What Kind of Reward?

Hugs

A simple hug or special one-on-one attention is often just as nice as a new toy or a chocolate bar. Sometimes, in our materialistic society, we forget that love is more important than anything. And it only costs time.

Praise

This is like a hug. A child loves to be praised. He's done something right. At last! Don't *you* like being told when you get something right?

Star Chart

This is nice and straightforward for toddlers. Every time they sleep through the night or go straight to bed, they get a star. Pin the chart on the kitchen wall or somewhere where they can see it. When adults visit, point it out and make your child feel good. When your child reaches a certain number of stars, you could reward him with a small present.

Reward Box

To appeal to older children who think star charts are babyish, leave a small shoebox under your child's bed. If he stays quiet through the night, you can slip a small "reward" inside, such as a crayon or coloring book. If he doesn't stay quiet through the night, it will remain disappointingly empty . . .

Special Treat

Verbal promises mean more to children 5 years and older. Has your child wanted to do something, such as go to the playground? Promise to take him there if he is quiet through the night for 1 week. Buy him a new pair of pajamas—another reason to go to bed fast. (Be sure to follow through with your reward!)

It's not bribery. Actually, it's a reward for good behavior. And if it gets you there in the end, it's worth it. (Make sure your child always has to do a little more to achieve the same reward—otherwise no progress will be made.)

Positive Discipline

Positive discipline goes hand-in-hand with giving your child a reward. Positive discipline is about straightening out poor behavior.

For Example

☆ If your child went to bed a half-hour later than you asked him to, he has to go to bed a half-hour earlier the next night to make up for it. In other words, he has to pay himself back. Even toddlers can be taught to do this.

☆ If your child has disturbed you by yelling, he has to be particularly quiet on another occasion to make up for his earlier noise.

☆ If your toddler upset you by yelling or crying, he has to do something to make you feel better. This can be something as simple as drawing you a picture. It helps him see the point.

8

If All Else Fails

It doesn't work. You've tried to let your baby settle down in the middle of the night by himself, but he wouldn't. Your toddler started wandering around the house at 2 A.M. and wouldn't go back to his own bed. When you took him into yours, he wiggled all night. Your 4-year-old woke up at 4 A.M. and wouldn't go back to sleep.

To Spank or Not to Spank?

It's tempting. You've put your child to bed *and he keeps coming back downstairs*. You've run out of patience. You feel like giving him a good spanking. What's wrong with that?

Spanking doesn't make anyone happy. You want bedtime to be a pleasant time—but if you spank your child, he won't be happy. And he won't go to bed in the right frame of mind. He also learns to associate bedtime with something unpleasant.

If you spank your child, chances are you'll feel guilty afterward. Then you might overcompensate by giving in. "I shouldn't have hit my child like that. I'll let him stay up later until we've made up."

Emotions are contagious. When you get angry, your child gets angry too. You both lose control and then you are back to square one.

Stop yourself from getting angry by watching out for the danger signs. Some danger signs are when you

✧ Say things more than twice.

✧ Feel yourself getting upset.

✧ Say things you don't really mean.

Give yourself some breathing room and do the following:

✧ Go to the bathroom for a few minutes.

✧ Wash your face.

✧ Leave the room for a minute.

If the suggestions above don't work, you can

✧ Call it a day and give in. Let your child come downstairs or play. Put him to bed later. But when you do that, you are borrowing from the bank loan we talked about on page 62. You are borrowing time *and* patience. In the long run, it will take you *longer* to persuade your child that you are in charge.

✧ Decide to get angry, but in a controlled way. Remember chapter 3, about keeping your child in bed? You pretended you were an actor. You practiced putting on a serious face that said, "I mean what I say." Now put those acting lessons into practice. Look as though you mean what you're saying. "Bed. Now!" And remember—it's not negotiable.

John

John's parents always found him difficult to handle; he was always crying. When he was 2 years old, he did the opposite of what he was told. The only way they got John to do what they wanted was either to shout at him or spank him. The doctor explained it is normal for 2-year-old children to do the opposite of what they are asked to. This is called negativism. *John continued to be miserable and difficult, and his parents felt they had to spank him or shout to get him to behave. John was particularly difficult in the evenings, and he was spanked the most then.*

By age 4, John had become really difficult to manage. He had been expelled from daycare because he hit the other children. The situation became so serious that the parents saw a specialist. The specialist explained that every time they spanked John it likely made him to be more aggressive and difficult in the future. Even though it might be effective in the short term, a different system of reward that concentrated on teaching him to behave well would have long-term benefits.

Spanking teaches children what not to do, but does not help them know what to do. John's father designed a chart for the kitchen wall. The chart was marked off in half-hour periods, from 4 P.M. to 6:30 P.M. (bedtime). The parents cut out some small, colored stars and whenever John was obedient he was allowed to glue a star on his chart. John enjoyed this and became very proud of his chart, with all the colorful stars. Gradually, he became a much happier boy. His parents decided never to spank him again and they tried not to yell, either.

It's Not Working—What Do I Do?

Take a break if you feel unable to keep trying or to start again. Forget it for a while! Go back to what you did before. But do this for only a short time until you can summon enough energy to make a fresh start. Then try again.

Start Again

Take stock

Look at the questionnaire (pages 14 to 20) again. Pinpoint areas that worked and try again. Maybe you need practice as much as your child does. Perhaps you need convincing, too. So remember: Practice makes perfect.

Can anyone else do a better job?

As a parent, it's tempting to think you're indispensable. No one else could calm your child in the middle of the night. Or could they? If you have a grandparent, aunt, baby-sitter, close friend—tell them about your nighttime problems.

Ask them to watch your baby, toddler or older child for a few nights—preferably in your own house where the child knows the layout. Your "substitute parent" might have some bright ideas you've been too tired or impatient to think of. It's amazing what a fresh eye can see!

Start a self-help group

Talk to other parents. Ask your doctor or healthcare practitioner to put you in touch with other families whose children don't sleep. Get together and share your experiences. Maybe one of them has a good idea that might help you, and vice-versa.

Read this book together and follow the guidelines. There's power in numbers—give each other emotional support and compare notes.

Give Yourself an "Alternative" Helping Hand

Sometimes alternative remedies can help overcome sleeplessness. They might work for you in conjunction with some of this book's suggestions. Consult your local alternative or holistic practitioner for additional advice. (Always keep your doctor informed of any alternative remedies you intend to use.) Contact the following associations for more information:

American Holistic Health Association
PO Box 17400
Anaheim, CA 92817-7400
(714) 779-6152

American Holistic Medical Association
4101 Lake Boone Trail, Suite 201
Raleigh, NC 27607
(919) 787-5146

The following approaches and remedies can help:

Lavender oil

Buy this from a health-food store. Use it in very small quantities, according to the instructions. Try dabbing some on your child's skin—usually behind the ears—or on the bed sheets. Check the bottle's instructions, or call an aromatherapist to make sure the product is suitable for your child's age group.

Homeopathy

Visit an alternative-health practitioner for homeopathic remedies appropriate for your child's symptoms. The type will depend on your child's needs. For more information, contact:

National Center for Homeopathy
801 N. Fairfax Street
Suite 306
Alexandria, VA 22314
(703) 548-7790

Massage

You can massage your baby or toddler with oil as part of his bedtime routine. Massage can relax him and help him feel better about going to bed. (Again, consult with an aromatherapist or alternative healthcare practitioner before choosing an appropriate oil.)

9

Breaking
the Routine

Rigid bedtime patterns and routines are great, but sooner or later, something happens to break them. Usually these breaks are temporary, caused by minor illness or vacation. Always try to get back to normal as soon as you can, before new habits set in. Other breaks in routine, such as your child's daytime nap, may be more frequent.

Daytime Napping

Babies' nap habits vary tremendously. If you listen to other mothers, you may worry and wonder why your child isn't doing the same as their children. All babies are different, just as you differ from other parents. It would be a boring world if we were all the same!

Some babies sleep deeply for 3 or even 4 hours at a time during the day. Others wake far more often. Children between 6 months old and 1 year old stay awake for most of the day and get by with 1 or 2 naps. There's nothing wrong with that. It gives you time to do everything else you need to. Until, that is, you want to start a more regular bedtime routine.

The following chart shows the amount of time babies and toddlers usually sleep during the day.

Nap Chart		
Age	Frequency	Total Nap Hours Per Day
4-6 months	2-3 / day	3-7 hours
6-12 months	1-2 / day	1-6 hours
2 years	1 / day	1-3 hours
4 years	4 / week	1-3 hours

Developing Baby's Nap Routine

When developing a good nap routine, the goal is to not affect the
bedtime routine. Encourage your older baby to have his first nap
as soon as possible in the morning.
You might take him for a walk in
his stroller or even a ride in the
car so the motion helps him fall
asleep.

> When developing a good nap
> routine, the goal is to not affect
> the bedtime routine.

If he has a second nap, make sure it's either before or soon
after lunch (wait until his food has settled). Keep it short—wake
him after an hour or so. The longer the gap between the end of
his final nap and bedtime, the more willing he'll be to go to bed.
Make sure he is not getting overtired before bedtime.

If you put your baby to bed too early in the evening, he is
more likely to wake up earlier. If you put him to bed later in the
evening—such as between 8 and 10 P.M.—his sleeping hours are
more likely to coincide with yours.

At this stage, it's very much a matter of trial and error. If your
attempt doesn't work, try putting him down for his nap and final
sleep at different times until you've both worked out a pattern.

Did you know?

If children have a nap, they develop a longer attention span,
are happier and more relaxed.

Naps and Older Children

Your toddler reaches a tricky stage between the ages of 2 and 3. He may get grumpy and overtired if he doesn't have a nap. But if he *does* have a nap—even a short one—he won't feel like going to bed until much later in the evening. Some parents joke that a 20-minute nap is worth 3 hours of nighttime sleep. In other words, if your child naps for 20 minutes, it costs *you* 3 hours that night!

If you have older children you need to take or pick up from somewhere in the afternoon, your toddler may fall asleep in the car. Then he wakes up, full of life, at 5 P.M. Bang—there goes your evening!

What to do

✧ If your toddler gets really tired and upset because he doesn't have a daytime nap, his body is telling you he genuinely needs more rest—even if it doesn't fit your schedule. Make his nap as early as possible in the afternoon by putting him down in his crib or bed.

✧ Move up your daytime routine. If your toddler is overtired without a daytime nap and is so exhausted that he falls asleep at dinner, move up dinner to 5 P.M. and bed at 6 P.M.

✧ Rethink your day. Is it possible for someone else to bring home your older child in the afternoon? That way, your toddler won't fall asleep when you pick up older siblings. If someone wants to meet you in the afternoon and you know your younger children will fall asleep on the way back, see if you can meet earlier in the day instead. Or ask your friend to come to your house instead.

This might sound as though you're planning your life around your child's, but it's only until his body clock learns to manage without daytime sleep.

Summer and Winter Schedules

Just when your child gets into a routine, the clocks change. Suddenly, it's an hour later or an hour earlier than yesterday. It's hard even for some adults to cope with this change. Imagine what it's like for your child!

What to do

⚝ Do nothing differently for older babies and younger toddlers. Stick to your usual routine at the (new) time by the clock on their bedroom wall. There's no need for them to realize anything is different. Young children adapt quickly to changing bedtime by an hour.

⚝ Use the clock for older and more streetwise toddlers and children. When they say, "Why do I have to go to bed? It's still light outside," point to the clock. Explain the time change in simple terms. For example, "Now it's summer. It's lighter, but it's still time to go to bed. Look at the clock. You always go to bed at 7 P.M."

⚝ Buy heavier curtains to shut out the light. A cheaper option is to buy a pair of curtain liners, which you hang between the curtain and the window to make your child's bedroom darker. They are available from most fabric stores.

Baby-sitters

At last! You're going out for the evening. You haven't had a night off for months. But will your baby-sitter be able to get your child to bed happily?

Going out for the evening is a double-edged sword. You want to get out, but on the other hand, you don't. What if your child can't go to sleep without you? Will a baby-sitter destroy the routine you have so carefully built? Relax! One night won't spoil everything. But you can make things go as smoothly as possible.

What to do

⚝ Make sure your baby-sitter is mature, reliable, experienced and has references (always check them).

⚝ Write down your contact number on the kitchen memo board or on the phone book: A flimsy scrap of paper might get lost. Also, leave another contact number for emergencies in case the sitter can't reach you.

⚝ Introduce your sitter to your children at least once and preferably several times before your night out. Even if your baby is too young to recognize her, it gives your sitter a chance to get familiar with your family. Watch how your sitter holds, plays with and talks to your child. If she's more interested in how the television works or her pay, think twice about hiring this person to baby-sit.

✧ Explain your child's bedtime routine to your sitter. Also write it down clearly (6:00 Bath, 6:15 Story, 6:30 Lights out). Give her the "magic" bedtime phrase such as "Goodnight, sleep tight." It reassures your child. Leave out stuffed animals and explain where the drinks and snacks are.

✧ Ask your sitter to stick to the routine as closely as possible. If your child seems very upset without you, let her adapt it accordingly. For example, she may need to stay by your child's bed instead of saying goodnight and leaving the room as you have learned to do.

✧ Put babies and younger toddlers to bed *before* you go out. Explain to older toddlers and children that your sitter will be there if they wake up. It can be terrifying for a child to wake up and find someone else is there if you haven't warned them about this in advance.

✧ Don't stay out too long when using a sitter for the first time.

✧ If you're leaving your children with a friend, explain the routine anyway. Tell your friend how important the routine is to you. But also remember it might be more difficult for a friend to stick to this, especially if she has children of her own. It's only one evening—as we've said, routines can sometimes be broken. The important point is to make sure they are not broken too often.

George

Before he was born, George's parents used to like going out and meeting friends in the evenings. After his birth, they could not afford a regular baby-sitter, so they decided to take George along when they went out. They were surprised how easy it was to put George into the carrier and take him anywhere at night. He would relax surprisingly well—until he was about 7 months old. Then it became progressively more difficult to get him settled—he didn't like strangers or unfamiliar places.

Their doctor said this was not surprising, because at the age of 6 to 8 months children begin to recognize the outside world and distinguish between what is familiar and what is strange. They develop "stranger anxiety." In most cases it disappears between the ages of 3 and 4. Then you can again take children with you for an evening out. They are usually not a problem—provided they are given clear instructions about what they can and can't do and as long as they have a comfortable bed to sleep in.

Going on Vacation

You've been looking forward to your vacation for so long but now you are full of doubt. Will your child be able to sleep on the plane, or will he run around annoying everyone? Will you be able to keep him awake on the car trip so he goes to bed at the normal time when you reach your destination? Will the bed or crib at your vacation destination be safe?

Sleep During the Trip

Sometimes it helps if your baby, toddler or older child sleeps on the way. It might disrupt his evening bedtime routine, but it's only for one night. If you've already established a good pattern, this is unlikely to undermine it.

Pack a Travel Bag with Sleep in Mind

Make sure you have all the necessary sleep "accessories" for your child's routine (stuffed animals, bedtime storybook, blanket, and so on). When you reach your destination, you'll have everything ready instead of having to search through bulging suitcases on the hotel floor or in the car trunk.

Tip ✶

🌙 To keep your older toddler or child awake during the trip, pack a surprise bag of goodies to keep him from falling asleep. Put in a coloring book, crayons, magic drawing board or simple puzzles, for example.

The Vacation Bedroom

If you use a travel agency, ask them to check that the crib or bed conforms to U.S. or Canadian safety standards. (See the appendix for more information.) When you arrive at your destination, check the crib carefully for loose bolts or anything your child could swallow.

✿ Does the mattress fit snugly, or could your child's face get trapped between the mattress and frame?

✿ Are the bars on the crib wide enough for your child to get stuck between? Is the crib on casters? If so, it could move when you don't want it to.

✿ Is the bedroom safe? Could your child fall out the window or off the balcony? Are there bumps, cracks or edges on the floor he might trip over?

Sometimes you can improvise:

✿ Secure the crib between 2 single beds so it can't move.

✿ Put furniture obstacles in place so your child can't get onto the balcony. Consult the hotel manager if you're worried.

Tip ✶

🌙 To reassure your child, take his own blanket to make the crib or bed feel more like his bed at home.

Have Fun

Vacation is supposed to be fun, so enjoy your break! At the same time, try to stick to your child's routine without being a stick-in-the-mud. If you want to go out to eat in the evening but your child is usually asleep by 8 P.M., try eating earlier. If he normally has an afternoon nap but you want to go out, take the stroller so he can still get his sleep.

Back to Normal

When you come home from vacation, get back into your bedtime routine as soon as possible. Hopefully, you won't have deviated from it too much anyway.

School Vacation

If you have older children at school, it's tempting to let them sleep in later than usual during vacation. The problem is you might do the same and your younger ones might, too—especially if bedtime is later because there isn't school the next day.

By the time the new school year arrives, everyone needs to go to bed on time—but your routine might have fallen by the wayside! The following ideas can help:

- Stick closely to what you usually do, but allow older children more leeway. For example, they could stay up (or sleep in) a half-hour longer than usual. Don't let it become much longer or it will be more difficult to get back to the old sleep cycle. Keep the usual boundaries for younger children.

- A week before the new semester starts, go back to the old routine. If it doesn't work, you've got time to fix it before the semester actually begins.

10

Older Children

When your children are small, you assume life will get easier when they reach the age of 5. They'll be able to feed themselves, take themselves to the bathroom, go to school and sleep through the night.

Perhaps it's just as well you don't find out the truth until they get to that age. Otherwise, you might not have the strength to go on! The truth is, children can continue to have sleep problems into their teenage years and even into adulthood.

How Much Sleep Does Your Older Child Need?

Older children tend to go through phases of sleeping for longer periods than they did when they were younger. They might sleep for more than 12 hours. On the other hand, older children sometimes get a buzz out of *not* sleeping.

> *Tip* ★ ★ ★ ★ ★ ★ ★ ★ ★ ★ ★ ★ ★ ★ ★ ★ ★ ★
>
> If your younger children are already in bed, use this "spare" time as a special time to talk to your older children before they turn out the lights.

Older children sometimes feel neglected because Mom is paying more attention to younger siblings. Now the little ones are in bed, there's time to give older kids extra one-on-one attention— even a few minutes is enough. Talk about the day over a cup of hot chocolate. Or dust off your old childhood books and read to your older children. Even though they can read themselves, they also enjoy someone else reading to them. It's part of a soothing wind-down bedtime routine.

You'll be surprised how much you can enjoy this special time. It brings you closer to your children during those awkward adolescent years. However, it is best to keep this special time short about, 5 to 10 minutes—so it ends while your child is still enjoying it and hasn't become bored.

Tip

Don't allow your child to have a television in his bedroom because

You can't be sure what your child is watching.

Bedrooms are intended for sleep.

If you allow your child to fall asleep watching television, it becomes a habit.

He might go to sleep without turning it off. (Leaving on electric appliances is dangerous because it is a fire hazard.)

Common Questions and Issues

"I don't want to go to bed."

Television becomes a real temptation for older children. Your child says, "All my friends watch it until 9 P.M., so why can't I?"

What to do

Stand by your own beliefs. Decide what you feel is the right bedtime and stick to it. Remember the routine you followed when your child was a toddler. Devise a routine suitable for your child's age, and stick to it. If bath time is 7:30 P.M. and bed 8 P.M., then bedtime stands, even if he does want to watch something at 8:30 P.M. (You can also tape a special program on the VCR to watch at another time.)

❧ Make a joke out of it. Point out adults who look tired or have heavy bags under their eyes. Ask your child if *he* wants to look like that. Remind your child he needs to sleep in order to grow.

"I can't sleep."

It's not a nice feeling to lie in bed, unable to sleep. You want to sleep, but you can't. As an adult, you probably recognize that you will fall asleep eventually. But it's a scary feeling for an older child.

What to do

❧ Tell him, "That's fine. You don't need to fall asleep—just rest."

❧ Don't encourage him to read or do something active. That's *not* resting. He's already had time to read a book before bedtime. Although there is nothing wrong with reading at night, it is not possible to read and go to sleep at the same time. Also, reading could become part of the sleep habit. Instead, encourage him to read another time.

❧ Encourage your child to review his day, backwards. This gets progressively more difficult—the morning seems like a long time away. That's good, because the effort in remembering makes him feel sleepier.

❧ Joke about it. Tell him to *try* to stay awake if he can't sleep.

❧ Is your child physically comfortable? Is he warm enough? Is his bed still suitable? If your older child is still sleeping in the bed he had as a 5- or 6-year-old, it might be too narrow or short. Maybe the mattress is lumpy. Maybe he needs a firmer one to support his increased body weight.

"I can't make my older child get up in the morning."

What to do

☆ Give him plenty of warning.

☆ Draw the curtains or turn on the light at least 10 minutes before he needs to get up.

☆ Point out that if he went to bed earlier, he'd wake up on time.

☆ Make sure he has a clock or a watch in his room. Make him responsible for his own time. If he's late for school, he will be the one to get a detention, not you . . .

Rules Are Made to Be Broken

Every now and then, it's fun to do something you shouldn't. There's no harm if your older child chats for half the night to a friend who is staying overnight. It's only once in a while, so don't be too hard on him. It's fun, after all.

The same goes for late nights. If your child goes out on a Saturday night, it's fine—providing you're happy with the circumstances. But he still needs to go to bed on time during the week when there's school the next day. And you still need to tell him firmly—just as you did when he was little, and even if he's as tall as you!

You feed him and provide a roof over his head. While he's in *your* house, he has to follow *your* rules. Don't be scared of telling him—but make it fun, too. Promise that when he has a house of his own and you come to stay, you'll follow *his* house rules!

11

Time
For You

Y ou might think your child's sleep is only important for him. It
helps him grow—physically and mentally. It teaches him independence. But good sleep habits for children are *also* vital to
you and the rest of the family.

We've already talked about how important it is to have an
evening on your own. This isn't being selfish. It's a basic need—
just as you need food and drink. Being a parent can be like working on an assembly line: You love the things you're making (in
other words, your children) and you want to do a good job. But
you have to put "parts" (clothes, food, drink and sleep) on them
all day long. You have to do the same jobs—day in and day out.

Like every laborer, you need a coffee break, a time to recharge
your batteries. But, unlike most factory workers, you don't have a
union to make sure you do. You have to take care of yourself.

Guide your children into a bedtime routine, and you'll be
able to set aside time for yourself. When things go wrong and you
feel like giving up and doing what your children want instead of
what *you* want, remember your goal.

You and Your Partner

You don't need time just for yourself. You also need time for your partner—or, if you don't have one, time to talk to other people and maybe go out. There's a joke that children are one of the best contraceptives available. Sadly, that's true, especially if your children regularly hop into bed with you or if they go to sleep in your bed!

It is important that you and your partner have time to enjoy each other, and continue a healthy sex life. Some parents take the opportunity to be intimate with each other even if their child is in bed with them. There will come a stage when your child is aware of what is going on. Even if you don't mind, it could well lead to embarrassing situations—especially when your little one goes to school and tells the teacher! In any case, it is a form of abuse to expose children to adult sexuality. It confuses them and encourages them to experiment themselves. Only you can decide which bedtime patterns are right for you and your family. But it's worth remembering all the pros and cons.

Common Questions and Issues

"We don't see things the same way."

When you first met your partner, you probably talked about the music you liked, the books you liked to read, where you came from and how many brothers and sisters you had.

It's not surprising that when you have a child, you may disagree about how you to bring him up. If he doesn't want to eat his dinner, one of you might think he should have to and the other might think he should be left alone.

The same goes for sleep. Maybe you think your wandering toddler should be firmly escorted back to bed, but your partner thinks he should be allowed to come into your bed so you can get some rest.

What to do

⟡ Talk about it.

⟡ See each other's point of view.

⟡ Try each other's methods out and see what works best.

✨ Remember you'll still need each other when your baby grows up and no longer needs you.

✨ Recall what brought you together in the first place and try to re-kindle that interest.

✨ Make a special effort when you are finally alone. Cook a candle-lit dinner or schedule a baby-sitter.

How to Wean Yourself from Your Child at Night

That's right: *It's not always the child who has to be weaned.* Often a parent who's especially close to a child has to learn to let go at night. He or she has to learn that a child can sleep safely on his own.

Maybe your child is the youngest and you have an understandable need to "baby" him more, or perhaps he's a very wanted child after a miscarriage or several years of trying.

It's not surprising you find it difficult to let go at night. If he cries, your immediate reaction is to rush in. When he's asleep, you might constantly check on him.

What to do

✨ Accept your feelings—they are natural.

✨ Make sure your child is healthy and his room is safe.

✨ Allow yourself to check on him at limited times—once during the evening and maybe once during the night. Reduce the frequency just as you reduced the amount of time you spent in his bedroom when he wanted you to stay.

✨ Remember you are helping him by encouraging him to establish a good sleep routine, just as you help him when you prepare a healthy meal or walk him down the street safely.

Your Own Sleep Patterns as a Child

It's true we sometimes carry our childhood experiences around with us like baggage. What was your own experience of sleeping when you were a child? If you were scared of the dark, chances are you might pass on these fears to your child. Stop yourself before it's too late! Remind yourself that being afraid of the dark didn't help you. Don't pass on the same legacy to your own children, who will pass it on to *their* children.

Were you forced to go to bed early when all your friends were allowed to watch television or listen to the radio? Perhaps the memories make you move in the opposite direction, away from routine. That's fine, if it's what you want. But think again. Was the routine harmful to you? Could you compromise and allow your child some freedom in the evening *and* keep him to the rules you want him to follow?

Did you have to share a room with a brother or sister? If so, you might have hated it. Perhaps you wanted your own space, so now you've put your own children in different rooms. Do they want to be apart? Would they enjoy each other's company and feel comforted by it? Or would they chat too much and disrupt each other's routine? Try different options and see what works for you.

> Try different options and see what works for you.

Your Health and Happiness

Your own health and happiness can deeply affect how well your child sleeps. Is it possible you might be depressed? If so, this might rub off on your children, who will find it hard to go to sleep. It can be difficult to think positively when you're trying to get them into a routine.

Don't be afraid to see a doctor. Depression nowadays is not a stigma. Many new parents—and old ones—feel low or are even clinically depressed. But you *can* do something about it. Your doctor can help you. (If he or she isn't sympathetic, find one who is.)

Conclusion

My Child Still Isn't Sleeping!

If you've read this book and your child still isn't sleeping, don't throw it across the room in a rage! Instead, remind yourself

☆ Sleeplessness in children is a common problem.

☆ Bringing up children is hard work but very rewarding.

You can always try again. Put away the book for a few weeks and then read it again. You or your child may have changed. You may be ready to tackle issues you couldn't tackle when you first tried.

Approximately 80% of parents who tried the Three-Day Sleep Plan (see chapter 4) found it created a big improvement in their children's sleep habits.

Making an Investment

Having a child is like putting your money into a savings account. You're making an investment in the future. You put time, effort and love into your child. One day, all your hard work pays off. It may take years—just like it takes years for interest on a savings account to build—but you will get there in the end.

Sometimes, you take out money from your savings. You could see this as deviating from the sleep routine once in awhile. It's all right. Enjoy breaking the rules every now and then. Then go back to the basics with ease and confidence. Or read this book again! Goodnight . . .

Appendix

For safety information for cribs, beds and other products for your child, contact the following agencies:

In the United States

Consumer Product Safety Commission
Washington, DC 2027
Tel: Consumer Hotline: (800) 638-2772
      TTY for the Hearing Impaired: (800) 638-8270
Website: http:\ \ www.cpsc.gov

In Canada

Federal Health Canada
Health Protection Branch
A.L. 0913A
Ottawa, Canada
K1A 0K9
Tel: (613) 957-2991
Website: http:\ \ www.hc-sc.gc.ca

Index